Arctic Peoples

Craig A. Doherty
Katherine M. Doherty

CHELSEA HOUSE
PUBLISHERS
An imprint of Infobase Publishing

✳ ✳ ✳

Arctic Peoples

Chelsea House
An imprint of Infobase Publishing
132 West 31st Street
New York NY 10001

Library of Congress Cataloging-in-Publication Data
Doherty, Craig A.
  Arctic peoples / Craig A. Doherty and Katherine M. Doherty.
    p. cm.—(Native America)
  Includes bibliographical references and index.
  ISBN 978-0-8160-5970-6 (alk. paper)
  1. Arctic peoples—History—Juvenile literature. 2. Arctic peoples—Social life and customs—Juvenile literature. I. Doherty, Katherine M. II. Title. III. Series.
  GN673.D66 2007
  971.9—dc22   2007013413

Chelsea House books are available at special discounts when purchased in bulk quantities for businesses, associations, institutions, or sales promotions. Please call our Special Sales Department in New York at (212) 967-8800 or (800) 322-8755.

You can find Chelsea House on the World Wide Web at
http://www.chelseahouse.com

Text design by Erika K. Arroyo
Cover design by Salvatore Luongo
Maps by Dale Williams

Printed in the United States of America

VB MSRF 10 9 8 7 6 5 4 3 2 1

This book is printed on acid-free paper and contains 30% post-consumer recycled content.

Note on Photos

Many of the illustrations and photographs used in this book are old, historical images. The quality of the prints is not always up to modern standards, as in some cases the originals are damaged. The content of the illustrations, however, made their inclusion important despite problems in reproduction.

*This book is dedicated to the many students of all ages
we have worked with and taught over the years.*

⁂

Craig and Katherine Doherty

⁂

Contents

Introduction

Native American peoples live and have lived for millennia throughout the Americas. Many people think of Indians solely in the past tense, as part of history. While these groups have a long and interesting history, their contributions to American society have continued through the 20th century and into the 21st century. Native America today is an exciting place, with much waiting to be discovered. This series of books will introduce readers to these cultures.

Thousands of years ago people from Asia migrated to the Western Hemisphere and spread throughout the lands that would later be called North and South America. Over the millennia, before Europeans found their way there, these peoples settled the Western Hemisphere, and a number of elaborate Native cultures developed. The Aztec, Maya, and Inca had large cities in North, Central, and South America. In what is now the United States, Pueblo groups in the Southwest and the Mound Builders in the Mississippi River basin lived in large towns and small cities. People lived in every corner of the land and adapted to every climatic condition, from the frozen Arctic home of the Inuit to the hot, dry desert inhabited by the Tohono O'odham of what is now southern Arizona and northern Mexico.

When in A.D. 1492 Christopher Columbus arrived in what Europeans would call the Americas, he mistakenly thought he was in the part of Asia known as the Indies. Columbus therefore called the people he encountered Indians. These Native Americans all had their own names for their many tribes; however, as a group they are still often referred to as American Indians or just

Indians. Each group of American Indians has its own story of how its ancestors were created and ended up in the group's traditional homelands. What is known about the Americas before the arrival of Europeans, however, has been determined mainly by studying the artifacts found at archaeological sites throughout the Americas. Despite the efforts of scientists from a wide variety of fields, there remain numerous questions about how these diverse cultures developed in North America. Scholars have a number of theories.

One part of the story that most people agree on is that present-day Native peoples of the Americas—including American Indians and Inuit—are descended from those who came to America from Asia. Many came on foot before the end of the last ice age, which ended about 10,000 years ago. Others, such as the Inuit, arrived much later as they spread out around the polar ice cap by boat and over the ice. Many sources refer to a "land bridge" that existed between what is now Siberia and Alaska and allowed the passage of people from Asia to North America. In many ways, this is a misleading term. During the last ice age, from about 40,000 years ago to 10,000 years ago, large sheets of ice called glaciers that were thousands of feet thick at times extended into North America as far as what is now the northern part of the United States. There was so much water locked into the glaciers that scientists estimate that the oceans were more than 400 feet lower than they are today.

The Bering Sea is the body of water that now lies between Siberia and Alaska. However, 400 feet beneath this sea is a land mass more than 1,000 miles wide. So, instead of talking about a

THE STUDY OF PALEO-INDIANS

Scientists from a variety of fields have worked to explain the origins of the more than 500 tribes that existed in North America at the end of the 15th century. The people who play the biggest role in this research are archaeologists. An archaeologist studies the past by finding objects called artifacts that people leave behind. Archaeologists refer to the earliest people in North America as Paleo-Indians. They use this term because they are studying people who lived during the Paleolithic period, or Old Stone Age, which existed from about 40,000 to 10,000 years ago in North America.

In addition to archaeologists digging up artifacts to study, other scientists contribute information about the plants, animals, climate, and geologic conditions that existed at the time. Still other scientists have developed numerous techniques to date the artifacts that the archaeologists dig up.

historical, narrow "land bridge" that facilitated the peopling of
the Americas, it is important to see the area that scientists now
refer to as Beringia as a wide, relatively flat plain that looked

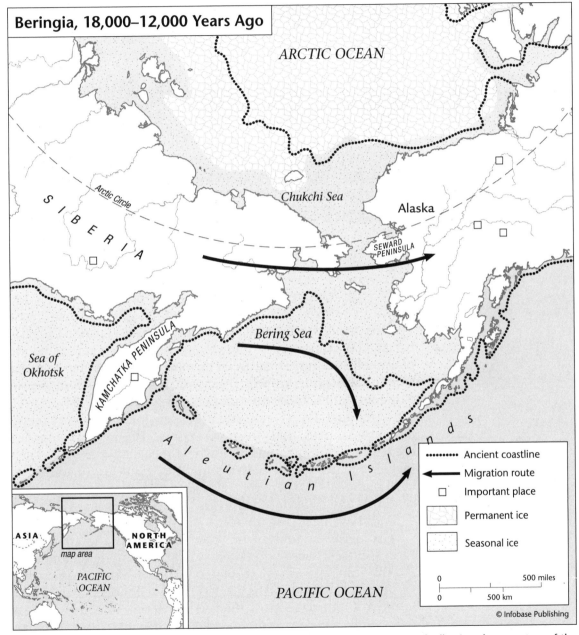

During the last ice age a wide plain between Asia and North America was exposed, allowing the ancestors of the
American Indians to cross to the Americas. These first Americans traveled over land and across the seasonal sea
ice that formed along the shoreline. Scientists refer to this area as Beringia, as it is now under the Bering Sea.

Glaciers, such as the one pictured here in the mountains of British Columbia, once covered most of the northern part of North America. *(Library of Congress, Prints and Photographs Division [LC-D4-14664])*

like the treeless tundra that still exists in the far north. Starting 25,000 years ago, or some would argue even earlier, bands of Paleolithic hunter-gatherers, people who lived by hunting animals and gathering wild plants, crossed Beringia, and the ice along its shores, to North America.

These first ancestors of the American Indians hunted many different animals that are now extinct. During this long ice age, many large mammals known as megafauna existed. They included mastodons, wooly mammoths, giant bison, and other large plant-eaters. There were also large predators such as American lions and saber-toothed tigers. The bones of many of these animals have been dug up at the campsites of Paleo-Indians.

Geologists, scientists who study the origins and changes in Earth's surface, believe that there was a period of time more than 23,000 years ago when people could have traveled down the Pacific coast. After that, the glaciers made it impossible for people to move south or to cross them. Then about 14,000 years ago, the coastal route was again open enough for migration. Approximately 11,500 years ago, the glacier in North America had melted to the point that there were two separate areas of ice. In the

West, much of the area from the mountains along the Pacific coast to the Rocky Mountains was covered by what is known as the Cordilleran ice sheet. In the East, ice covered the land in a continuous sheet from the Arctic Ocean south into what is today New England, New York, Ohio, Michigan, Wisconsin, Minnesota, and North and South Dakota. This is known as the Laurentide ice sheet. Between the two areas of glacier, there was an ice-free corridor from Alaska south into what is now the central plains of the United States. Many scientists agree that when this corridor opened, Paleo-Indians spread through the Americas.

Although most scientists agree on the major overland migration routes from Asia, some have suggested that Paleo-Indians may also have traveled down the Pacific coast of both North

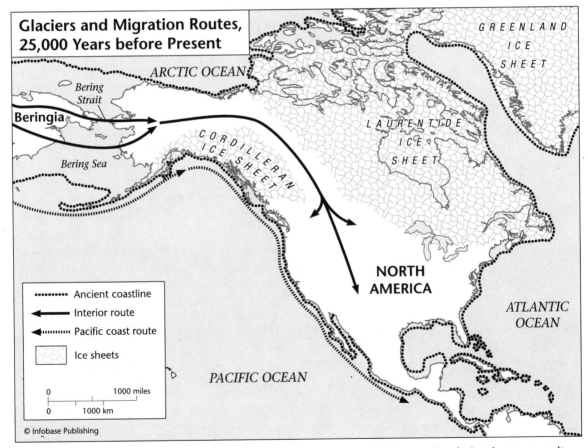

At first, people migrating from Asia lived in Beringia and what is now Alaska. As the glaciers began to melt, people were able to move south. The route along the Pacific coast opened up first, and then an ice-free area existed down through the North American plains.

and South America. They believe that boats may have been used by people who reached South America during these paleo-migrations. The fact that at least one site in southern Chile has been dated to at least 12,500 years ago would suggest that bands of people had spread out in the Americas well before the major migrations that appear to have taken place 11,500 years ago. The modern study of genetics has created speculation that one other possible route of migration existed during the Paleolithic period. Approximately 3 percent of American Indians share a genetic trait that is also found in parts of Europe. This has led to the idea that some people may have come from Europe by boat during Paleolithic times.

Most of what is believed about Paleo-Indians is very speculative because there are very few artifacts that have been found from these earliest Americans. It is now accepted, however, that as the glaciers receded, people spread through the Americas. They lived by hunting and gathering. It was once widely believed that these people lived primarily by hunting large

Large animals known as megafauna, such as the wooly mammoth pictured here, roamed North America during the last ice age and were hunted by Paleo-Indians. (© *Science VU/Visuals Unlimited*)

STONE TOOLS

Although in some areas of North America the American Indians made tools and decorative objects out of copper and the Inuit were known to make knives out of iron from recovered meteorites, the vast majority of tools were made of stone. Knives used for cutting, points for spears and arrows, as well as small blades and scrapers used in a variety of tasks were all made by flaking off pieces of a variety of types of stones. Flint, chert, and obsidian are all types of rock that flake apart when struck.

To make stone tools, the toolmaker started with a large piece of rock and hit it with a rock hammer. Large flakes of stone would break off and then be broken into smaller usable shapes and sizes. To remove smaller and smaller pieces as the tool was shaped and sharpened, different methods were applied. Often the toolmaker would use the point of an antler to apply pressure to a specific spot on the stone to remove a flake. Sometimes the antler was struck with a piece of wood until a flake of stone was removed. Other toolmakers applied pressure to the antler tip until the flake came off. As the edge took shape, smaller and smaller pieces were removed until the edge was extremely sharp. If the edge became dull, it could be reworked to sharpen it. The sites where usable stone is found often show that they were mined by Native Americans for thousands of years, going back to Paleo-Indian times.

animals such as the wooly mammoth and the giant bison. Although there are many archaeological sites that contain the bones of these large animals, it is now thought that these people also hunted many smaller animals and gathered the edible parts of many wild plants.

The original weapons of these early American Indians consisted of wooden spears with tips that had been hardened with fire. Some time after people were able to use the migration route in the center of North America, they began to attach stone points onto their spears. It is by the size and style of these stone points that archaeologists have been able to identify and group people into a number of paleocultural groups.

As archaeologists discovered early sites of human occupation in North America, they noticed that different groups used different shaped tools. These groups were usually named after the location of the sites where their artifacts were first found. Three of these earliest groups were first discovered in New Mexico, and one was found in Texas. Evidence of the New Mexico groups was first found near the towns of Clovis and Folsom, and the third group was found in the Sandia Mountains east of Albuquerque. The fourth group was first discovered near Plainview,

Clovis-style stone spear points are found in many locations throughout North America, indicating a relationship between early hunter-gatherer groups. *(Photo courtesy of Pete Bostrom)*

Texas, and is referred to as the Plano culture. Each of these groups had its own unique style of making their stone spear points; therefore, archaeologists can easily identify a Clovis- or Folsom-style spear point wherever it is found.

As the glaciers continued to recede, the people of these groups spread out in search of animals to hunt and plants to gather. Clovis-style spear points have been found throughout much of North America, and at one time scientists believed the Clovis people were the first North Americans. It is now known that the earliest Clovis sites date to about 11,500 years ago and that people were in the Americas long before that. Some people suggest that the Clovis people were a new wave of migration into the Americas. Others think that they had been in Alaska for a long time and moved south about this time as travel became possible down the center of North America. It may never be known which theories are accurate.

What is known for certain is that these early culture groups in the center of the continent spread east, west, and south. It is also known that the climate began to change. Between 10,000 and 5,000 B.C., North America went from the Ice Age with its large Pleistocene (time period from 1.6 million to 10,000 years ago) animals, like the saber-toothed tiger and wooly mammoth, to the climate and landscape that exists today. The Paleo-Indians that existed at the beginning of this time learned from generation to generation to adapt to changes in their environment.

Over thousands of years between the end of the last ice age and the coming of Europeans to North America, the different cultures of American Indians developed along a number of lines. As the climate became less severe, American Indians spread out to cover the entire continent. They created new technologies to deal with the vastly different environments that they encountered. By the end of this time, the American Indians had broken into distinct language groups and eventually into a wide variety of tribes.

Modern researchers divided North America, excluding Mexico, into 10 cultural regions, known as culture areas, to aid in their study of American Indians. In classifying these areas, scientists took many factors into account. Among those were similarity in culture, environment, and geography. Within a culture area there may be a number of tribes that speak languages that differ, however, the way they have adapted to the geography of the region gave groups many similarities. For example, in the California Culture Area almost all groups used acorns as a major source of food. Therefore, they all had similar technology for harvesting, processing, cooking, and preserving acorns. In the Plateau Culture Area the prolific runs of salmon in the many rivers of the region became the primary food source and focus of the culture. Each of the ten regions has similar unifying aspects.

In some of these culture areas, however, there are numerous distinctions that can be made between groups in the region. For instance, in the Southwest, two distinct cultures live side by side within one culture area. One group known as Pueblo Indians (*pueblo* is the Spanish word for "town") lived in towns and were primarily farmers: Others consisted of various groups, such as

Acoma Pueblo in New Mexico is the oldest continuously inhabited community in the United States. Pueblo people have lived in Acoma for more than 1,000 years. *(Library of Congress, Prints and Photographs Division [LC-USZ62-74105])*

During World War II, the U.S. Army recruited members of the Navajo (Dineh) tribe to create a code using Navajo to transmit sensitive messages. This code proved indecipherable to enemies. *(Official U.S. Marine Corps photo USMC #69896/National Archives and Records Administration)*

the related Navajo (Dineh) and Apache, who were seminomadic and depended much more on hunting and gathering than on agriculture. In this region, the unifying aspect is more closely related to geography and climate of the region.

The culture areas that most scientists agree on are the Northeast, Southeast, Great Plains, Great Basin, Plateau, Southwest, California, Northwest Coast, Subarctic, and Arctic. Each volume in this series will show how the peoples in a culture area developed their distinct way of life, making the transition from Ice Age hunters/gatherers to the complex tribal cultures that existed when Christopher Columbus landed in the Caribbean in 1492. The lifeways and material culture of these people will be described in depth. Spiritual beliefs and social structure are also explained. Furthermore, readers will learn of the wide variety of housing and transportation developed for each region. Clothing and everyday items will be described, as will hunting, fishing, farming, and cooking practices. Readers will also learn how the American Indians fought to survive the long invasion of European settlers that followed Columbus and explore how, despite the best attempts of Europeans to eliminate the American Indians almost everywhere they found them, many tribes persevered and continue to exist today.

The long and fascinating history of Indian peoples is described, illuminating the many contributions made by Indians and Indian cultures to the broader American culture. In the 20th century, Indians finally began to have some success in regaining some land and respect. Indian soldiers fought bravely in various wars the United States participated in. All American Indians finally gained citizenship. Protests starting in the 1950s and 1960s as well as the work of Indian leaders resulted in victories in the courts and legislative chambers of North America. Increased pride in their heritage and a resurgence of Indian cultures have given many American Indians an optimistic outlook for the future as the 21st century unfolds.

The Last Arrivals

The ancient ancestors of the American Indians migrated from Asia at various times in the past. When exactly the first people crossed Beringia from Asia to North America is still a subject of debate among scholars. There is at least one archaeological site that indicates that there were people in the far northern reaches of North America as early as 25,000 B.C.

DATING ARTIFACTS

Scientists use a number of methods to determine the age of an archaeological site. One of the most often used is the carbon-14 method. All living organisms have a known amount of carbon-14 molecules. When the organism dies, carbon-14 begins to disintegrate at a rate that is also known. By measuring the amount of carbon 14 in a piece of wood or bone uncovered at an archaeological site, scientists can tell when that wood was cut from a living tree or when the animal died. Although conditions of the material and the site can cause a certain amount of error, carbon-14 dating is very important in determining the age of a site.

Scientists use other methods as well. The depth and number of layers of sediment at a site can help a geologist determine how long ago an artifact was left at a site. This method is called geochronology. To date more recent sites, scientists have developed a time line based on the pattern created by the growth rings of certain types of trees. This is referred to as dendrochronology. By overlapping a large number of samples, they have been able to extend the dendrochronological time line back almost 4,000 years. Scientists can also tell when an obsidian stone tool was made by measuring the amount of moisture that has escaped from the stone. This is known as obsidian hydration dating.

Prehistoric artifacts, such as this whalebone mask found at Izembek Lagoon on the western Alaska peninsula, provide clues about the lives of prehistoric Inuit and Alaska Natives. *(Anchorage Museum)*

This site is located along the Old Crow River in Canada near the Canada-Alaska border. Scientists have found bones of animals there that appear to have been marked by human tools. Radiocarbon dating estimates indicate those animals died approximately 27,000 years ago.

Although people appear to have been in the north long, long ago, the ancestors of the Aleut and Inuit people of the Arctic are fairly recent arrivals in North America. Scientists have broken down the settlement of the Arctic Culture Area into five stages that start at 25,000 B.C. and take the prehistory of the region up to A.D. 1800. Around 1800, European contact became fairly regular in the Arctic and from that point forward, there is a written record of the people of the far north. In the Arctic, the Native people, even though they experienced numerous changes due to the influence of European goods and technology, did not face the pressure from colonists that radically changed the face of Native America to the south.

STAGE 1:
25,000 to 5,000 B.C.

The earliest people in the Arctic region appear to have passed through the region as they followed large ice age animals such as mammoths and bison. It is possible that many of the artifacts they left behind are now at the bottom of the Bering Sea and will never be recovered and studied. In the Arctic and the Subarctic (the next culture area to the south of the Arctic), what has been found from the early parts of this period are mostly stone tools. These tools are often similar to those found in northeastern Siberia from the same time period. Scientists refer to the artifacts from these early sites as belonging to an American Paleo-Arctic tradition. Little is known about the people who made these tools. There is no evidence that people had spread across the Arctic during these early times. They seem to have moved inland where large herd animals were available for hunting.

During this long period, huge changes took place in the climate and geography of the North. As the ice age slowly came to an end, the glaciers began to melt and the oceans of the world began to rise. The last ice age is referred to as the Wisconsin Glaciation, and it ended about 10,000 years ago. By the end of this first stage in the cultural development of the Arctic, the land and water levels were very close to what they are today. It is around this time that scientists note the signs of a specific cultural group that eventually spread across the Arctic region.

STAGE 2:
5000 to 2200 B.C.

During this period, there seems to have been two areas of cultural development in the region. The first area is called Ocean Bay I and is centered on Kodiak Island and the nearby Alaskan peninsula. At about the same time in northern Alaska, the Northern Archaic culture was developing. These two early Arctic groups seem to have been fairly recent arrivals from Asia and probably crossed on the winter ice and by boat. This late migration may explain why there are physical differences between the two Arctic groups, Aleut and Inuit, and most other American Indians. It was during Stage 2 that the people of Arctic began to develop a unique culture.

There is still some disagreement between archaeologists as to the relationship of these sites and some Stage 1 sites. However, most agree that these two early Arctic groups seem to have been fairly recent arrivals from Asia and probably crossed on the winter ice and by boat.

STAGE 3:
2200 to 1200 B.C.

During this stage in the development of the Arctic culture, there was a split between the people known today as the Aleut

PHYSICAL ATTRIBUTES OF
ALEUT AND INUIT PEOPLE

When examining the physical aspects of a group of people, scientists take into account two types of attributes. They look at the genetic heritage of a group as well as changes that may have come about over many generations due to diet and habitat. The Aleut and Inuit have both genetic and ecological adaptations that set them apart from most other American Indians.

Genetically, researchers have determined that although all Native Americans share common ancestors in Asia, they can be separated by how far back that connection dates. The Aleut and Inuit are more closely related to groups in northeast Asia than they are to the Algonquian tribes of the Subarctic and Northeast culture areas. However, the Athabascan tribes of the Subarctic and their relatives the Navajo and Apache who migrated to the Southwest are fairly close genetic relatives of the people of the Arctic.

One physical distinction that is more apparent among Arctic people is the epicanthic eye fold, when the skin of the upper eyelid folds over making the eyelid appear to have a slant to it. The Aleut and Inuit share this trait with many Asian people. In addition, the people of the Arctic tend to be shorter and stockier than other Native American groups. In addition to these genetically inherited traits, scientists have documented a number of unique physical traits that they believe have come about as adaptations to the unique diet and environment of the Arctic.

The traditional diet of Aleut and Inuit people is almost entirely meat. Most of that meat came from marine mammals, fish, and caribou. After many generations of eating this high protein and high fat diet, the people of the Arctic's digestive systems learned to efficiently meet all the body's needs. Their bodies also evolved to more readily deal with the cold of the North.

Conserving the heat generated by the body is critical to survival in the extreme cold of the Arctic winter. The people of the Arctic display some unique physical adaptations that make them better suited to the cold. Scientific studies have shown that the basal metabolic rate, the body's ability to produce heat, is 13 to 33 percent higher among the Inuit than among non-Inuit people. They also have fewer sweat glands, which offer the major way the body lowers its temperature. It has also been determined that the blood vessels in their hands dilate (get larger) more quickly than other people's when they are exposed to cold. This allows more blood to flow into the hands and lessens the effect of the cold.

The Inuit and Aleut have several physical traits that may be a result of adaptations to the harsh climate of the Arctic. Kila, an Inuit woman from Coronation Gulf, Northwest Territories (now Nunavut), poses for a 1916 photograph. *(National Archives of Canada)*

and the Inuit. The Aleut are centered in the Aleutian Islands that stretch in an arc between Alaska and Siberia and form the southern boundary of the Bering Sea. The Inuit settled primarily along the coast of the mainland and the islands to the north of the Arctic coast. It was during this stage that the Inuit expanded across the north until they inhabited the Arctic from Siberia to Greenland, an area that is more than 6,000 miles from one end to the other.

Across the Arctic, scientists have given different names to the developmental stages of Inuit culture. In the Kodiak region, Stage 3 is referred to as the Takli Culture. Along the Bering Sea coast and in northern Alaska, the artifacts from this period fit into the Arctic Small Tool tradition. In Canada, the terms used are Independence I and pre-Dorset. In Greenland, terms used are Independence I and Sarqaq. Although there are different names, for the most part, Arctic Culture was developing in a linear fashion. Most of the people lived along the coast and sea mammals such as whales, seals, and walruses became more and more important as a source of subsistence.

What is known of all these early stages comes from the artifacts that have been found. During Stage 3, the tools became more specialized and showed a higher degree of craftsmanship. Many believe that the Aleut and Inuit languages began to diverge as the Aleut remained isolated offshore during this period. Although an Inuit in Greenland would not be able to understand the language of an Inuit from Alaska, both groups and all those in the Arctic in between speak languages with many similarities.

STAGE 4:

1200 B.C. to A.D. 600

During this stage, the people of the Arctic began to settle in larger and more permanent villages. The village at Point Hope, Alaska, from this time period had 600 houses, although some people do not think they were all lived in at the same time. The artifacts found from this stage of development include new technology such as pottery and whale oil lamps. There was also some use of copper and iron by Copper Inuit during this stage.

Again, scientists have given a variety of names to the advancing culture of the Inuit during Stage 4. In the Kodiak

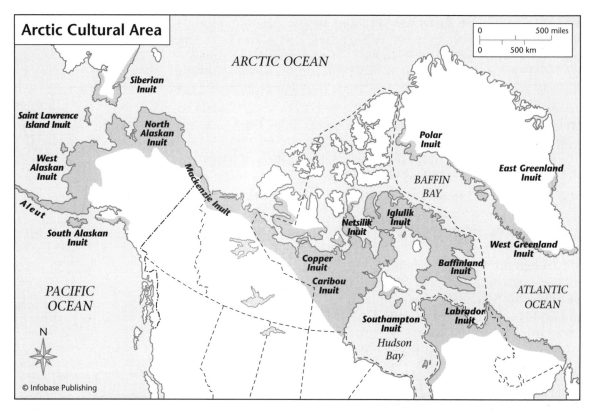

The Arctic Cultural Area stretches for 6,000 miles across the northern top of Siberia, Alaska, Canada, and Greenland. All the Native peoples of the area are descended from the same Asian ancestors. In the past they broke into two primary groups—the Aleut of the Aleutian Islands and the Inuit who live in the rest of the area.

region, this period is known as the Kachemak tradition. Along the Bering Sea and in northern Alaska, it is referred to as the Norton tradition. In Canada and Greenland, this time is called Dorset.

STAGE 5:
A.D. 600 to 1800
The final prehistoric stage of development in the Arctic is generally referred to as the Thule tradition. During this time, Arctic culture became more uniform across the entire range of the Arctic from Siberia to Greenland. The parts of Arctic culture that most people are familiar with took their most recognizable form during this time. The use of dogs and sleds for transportation,

INUIT METALWORK

Although most Inuit and Aleut tools were made from stone, wood, or bones and antlers, the group known as the Copper Inuit also made tools out of metal. In their region, located in Canada along the Copper River and on Victoria Island, deposits of copper were found on the surface of the land. They learned to hammer nuggets of copper into points for arrows, harpoons, and spears. They also were known to make knives out of iron that they found. It is believed that the small amounts of iron they used came from meteors.

snow houses known as igloos, skin-covered boats called kayaks and umiaks, and clothing such as the parka are all parts of Inuit culture that many know.

Except for the Aleut whose culture developed differently to suit their unique island environment, the people of the Arctic had

Whale bones and piles of stones are among the ruins of a permanent house from ca. A.D. 1000. This dwelling is characteristic of what the Inuit built during the Thule tradition, which lasted from A.D. 600 to 1800. *(Northwest Territories)*

VIKINGS IN GREENLAND

There is no question that people from Scandinavia settled along the southwest coast of Greenland around A.D. 1000. The exact date of their arrival and what eventually happened to their descendants are subject to much speculation. The main problem in the study of these settlements has to do with the fact that many of the stories and legends about Greenland were not written down until much later. Most believe that a Norwegian named Eric the Red came from Iceland to Greenland with a large group of settlers around A.D. 985. It is believed that they came from Iceland in 25 ships and that 11 of the ships were lost in the crossing.

In Greenland, they set up two settlements along the southwest coast. These settlements grew to the point that scientists today have identified the sites of 250 farms at what is called the eastern settlement and another 80 at the western settlement. However, they believe that some of the inland sites were most likely only inhabited in the summer. The settlers brought sheep, cattle, goats, and a few horses with them. The animal herds and flocks did well on the lush grasses of Greenland. The two settlements continued for a few hundred years and there seems to have been a certain amount of contact between the Norse settlements and the Greenland Inuit to the north. The Norse settlers referred to the Inuit as "Skraellings" and described them as little people who lived as hunters.

The Norse settlements of Greenland traded the tusks of narwhals (a whale with a long tusk that projects out from its mouth) and walruses

In this 1820 engraving that represents early Scandinavian inhabitants of Greenland, a Scandinavian man holding a bow and arrow stands next to a Scandinavian woman who wears a papoose that cradles a child. Scandinavians first sailed to Greenland in approximately A.D. 985. *(National Archives of Canada)*

and fur from a variety of native animals back to Iceland for foods such as grain that they could not grow in Greenland. One of the biggest mysteries surrounding the Norse settlements in Greenland is why they disappeared during the 14th century. The most likely explanation has to do with climate. Earth went through a relatively warm period during the time the Norse were in Greenland. Starting around A.D. 1200, the climate became cooler and may have

a much more unified culture than the Indians of many of the other culture areas. Many people refer to the Thule tradition as the classical period of Arctic culture when the social, religious, and family structures developed into a strong and complex society.

caused serious problems for the farms and domestic animals in Greenland. Inuit legends suggest that conflict broke out between the Inuit and the Norse settlements and the Inuit wiped out the settlements. Others suggest that loss of contact with Europe contributed to the downfall of the Norse in Greenland. It seems likely that it was not just one problem but all of these factors and more that could have caused an end to the earliest European settlements in North America.

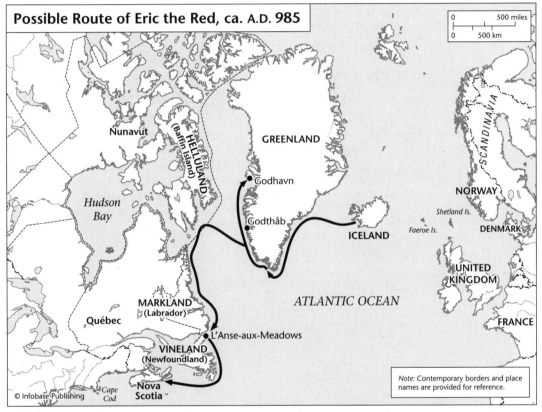

Possible Route of Eric the Red, ca. A.D. 985

Some time around A.D. 985 Scandinavian explorers and colonists left Iceland and sailed west. They established a colony on the west coast of Greenland and explored and briefly stayed on the northeastern tip of North America.

The fact that the Inuit lived in a land that was frozen solid for much of the year kept them insulated from the early invasion of European explorers and colonists that took place starting in the 15th century in the Caribbean and soon spread to the east coast of North America. The one major exception to that was in Greenland where Norse settlers from Iceland began arriving just prior to A.D. 1000.

When Europeans began to regularly travel to the Arctic for trade and exploration, they found a uniform culture inhabited by people they called Eskimos. Eskimo is an Algonquian word meaning "eaters of raw meat" and has now been replaced by the terms Inuit and Aleut, which are from the groups' own languages. Inuit means "the people" and Aleut is believed to mean "island." Although the Inuit and Aleut today have adopted many aspects of modern culture, they continue to have a connection to their ancestors as hunters and inhabitants of the frozen north.

2

Families and Tribal Groups

⚜ FAMILIES

Traditionally, the Aleut and Inuit people of the Arctic lived in a harsh environment that required the cooperation of everyone for survival. Among both groups, the family was most important. Everyone lived and worked within their family unit. Most groups were organized based on the male line of a family. For instance, in one of the large Aleut houses, several nuclear families would live together. This would usually include an older couple and their grown sons along with the wives and families of the sons. The men of the family would hunt together. When they hunted whales, they might be joined by the men of other households. In the largest Inuit communities, the men of a village might live in one or more separate houses known as a *kashim*.

Marriage was an important aspect of life in the Arctic. Girls would marry shortly after reaching puberty while young men would be three, four, or more years older before their first marriage. Because of the close relationship of the families in Arctic villages, young people often married relatives. It was considered taboo for people to marry their siblings or first cousins, but out of necessity more distant cousins often married. Although

Inuit society was traditionally organized around the family unit. An Inuit family composed of a mother, father, and son poses for a portrait taken in the early 1900s. *(Library of Congress, Prints and Photographs Division [LC-DIG-ppmsc-02276])*

11

LIFE IN A *KASHIM*

In the larger villages of the Arctic, the men often lived apart from their families in a men's lodge known as a *kashim*. Each male had his own space within the *kashim*. Where that space was in a lodge was determined by his position in the community. The leader of the *kashim* and the older males occupied the back wall furthest from the entrance. The men who were the heads of the community's households had their spaces along the side walls. The single men and young boys lived close to the entranceway.

The women of the community would bring food to the *kashim* to feed the men of their family as they were in charge of all the food after the men killed it and brought it to the women to butcher and preserve. The men kept their tools and weapons in the homes of their wives or mothers and might spend time at home during the day. Men would occasionally visit their wives during the night. Boys as young as five were sent to live with the men to begin their training to become hunters. The *kashim* was also used like a sweat lodge or modern-day sauna. Before European contact, the fire was built up until it became very hot in the *kashim*. Later, the people of the Arctic learned the Scandinavian custom of heating rocks with fire and then pouring water on the rocks to create steam.

Many communities were only big enough to have one *kashim* if any at all. However, in some of the larger villages, there were two or more *kashims*. When there were multiple *kashims*, there was often rivalry between them.

The wooden-plank doorway depicted in this early 1900s photograph leads to a *kashim*. A *kashim* was a building that traditionally housed Inuit men and also served as a sweat lodge and meeting place in larger Inuit villages. *(Library of Congress)*

In Inuit society sometimes men and women had multiple spouses. In this 1922 photograph, taken aboard the C.G.S. *Arctic*, Harold Grant holds Akpaliapik and crouches between Qlittalik and Puttiuq, the two wives of Takijualuk. *(National Archives of Canada)*

most people only had one husband or one wife, it was acceptable practice for a man or woman to have multiple spouses.

A man who was a very successful hunter might take a second wife because he could support her. In many cases, the second wife was the sister of the first wife. In some small villages, there was an imbalance between the number of adult men and women. If there were more men than women, a woman might take a second husband. Some marriages were arranged by the families. Others were agreed to by the man and woman. In some communities, when a young man wanted to marry, he would give the young woman's mother the furs needed to make a parka for the potential bride. If the woman wanted to accept the marriage proposal, she would bring a meal to her suitor in the *kashim*.

In most cases, the woman would move to her husband's family home, but before she did so, the new husband would have to pay a bride's fee. As the people of the Arctic had little in the way of excess goods to compensate a family for the loss of a daughter,

Inuit children were expected to learn skills that would enable them to help their families and community. Mukpi, the youngest survivor of the SS *Karluk,* which sank in the Arctic Ocean off Canada in 1914, smiles for this portrait. *(Library of Congress, Prints and Photographs Division [LC-DIG-ppmsc-02314])*

the husband would usually move in with his new wife's family and help support them for one to two years. The bride's fee usually ended on the birth of their first child.

Children were extremely important to the Arctic people. It was critical to the future well-being of the family that children grew and learned the skills they would need to help their families. As there was a strong division of labor between men and women, boys and girls had different skills to learn. The boys would start going with their fathers and uncles when they were young and would learn about hunting by observing. They would also practice hunting with small bows and arrows. In many Arctic communities, the first time a boy killed a seal on his own was considered the beginning of being an adult.

The girls had to learn domestic work such as the cooking, sewing, and helping care for younger siblings that was crucial to survival in the Arctic. By the time they reached puberty, they had to have mastered the skills they would need to start their own families. Puberty marked a girl's passage into adulthood and was accompanied by a certain amount of ceremony. Another celebration was held when a newborn baby was first shown to the community. In some communities, a woman would go off to a special hut when her baby was due, and would not come out until a few days after the baby was born. At the birth of a new child, the parents would give gifts to the rest of the community as a part of the celebration of the new life that had been created.

Children were raised within the household of their mothers and were treated with respect. Children were rarely punished

THE CREATION OF THE WORLD

Among the people of the Arctic, the first raven was considered the creator of their world and all that lived on it. For that reason, ravens are considered sacred birds to the Aleut and Inuit. When telling of raven and the creation of the world, different storytellers add different details and embellishments, but the basic facts of the story remain the same.

Long, long ago there was nothing but the sky and the snow that fell out of it. At one time, the great raven was soaring along and the snowflakes were collecting on his wings. When he tipped his wing down, the snow rolled toward the tip of his wing, forming into a ball. When the raven lifted his wing, the snowball rolled back toward his shoulder. Amused by this game, the raven continued until the snowball was too big for him to carry, so he flipped it into the air where more and more snow stuck to the ball as it spun. When it got very big, the raven landed on it.

When the raven landed, he lifted his beak to reveal a humanlike face. He then kicked at the snow and found that earth had formed under the snow. This gave the raven an idea and he lowered his beak and flew up into the sky and began spreading numerous seeds around the world he had created. As the plants began to grow, the raven noticed that there was one vine that was growing very quickly and a number of pods were developing on it.

The raven flew down to investigate. As he stared at the fast-growing plant, one of the pods began to wiggle. At first a foot came out, and then the body and the head of the first man appeared. The raven was somewhat surprised but was pleased to see a creature that looked like himself. The raven showed

For the people of the Arctic, the raven is a sacred symbol. Raven is described in some stories as the creator of all life, but in other stories he plays the role of a trickster. *(U.S. Fish and Wildlife Service)*

the man around the world he had created and soon realized that the man would need more than the plants that were now growing on the world.

The raven next decided to create a companion for the man and fashioned a woman from clay and gave it life. The raven then went on creating pairs of animals, birds, and fish from clay, giving them life as well. The raven then taught the man and woman the skills they would need to survive in the world. He showed them how to make fire and build houses. He created the Sun so there would be light sometimes. He taught the man to hunt and the woman the skills she needed. When the raven went back to the vine, more men came out of the pods. Raven made them companions as well. Some of the men moved to the edge of the land and hunted along the shore of the ocean and on the winter ice. Other men stayed further inland and learned to survive by hunting the caribou and other land animals.

(Author's note: This version of the creation myth was compiled by the author from a variety of sources.)

Family members raised Inuit children cooperatively. In this 1912 photograph, an Inuit woman wears a pack that holds a sleeping baby. *(Library of Congress, Prints and Photographs Division [LC-USZ62-101165])*

and were taught to be a part of the family community. They learned to respect their elders and old people in the family were cared for by all. The elders were respected for the knowledge they had accumulated over the many years of their lives. The people of a family rarely argued or fought. Survival of the group was too dependent on the cooperation of everyone for the group to survive if there was discord.

If there was a disagreement between two people in the community, the Aleut and Inuit had a unique way of solving the problem. The two people would have a public duel. However, in these duels, the only weapons were words. In some groups, the words were sung, in other groups they were just spoken. During the duel, the two people involved would take turns insulting each other. Each person was expected to sit and listen to the insults without showing anger. If a participant lost control, he or she lost the duel. If the two people who were angry at each other were from different villages, then the disagreement might lead to violence. There were often feuds that went on between different communities. Sometimes these violent feuds lasted for many years.

Despite occasional duels and feuds, people of the Arctic spent most of their time making sure they had enough of the essentials to survival. They had learned long ago that survival depended on cooperation and most people worked together for the welfare of their family first and then their community.

COMMUNITIES AND BANDS

When people talk about American Indians who live south of the Arctic region, they usually refer to people in terms of the tribe to which they belong. In the Arctic, the concept of a tribe is less valid. Among the Aleut and Inuit, the family was the most important unit. In a community, most of the people were related in some way and with the exception of moving to seasonal camps to fish or hunt, the people of the Arctic stayed in a very small area. In the past, many Arctic people would live their entire lives and never meet more than 100 different people. Among some groups, there were larger communities and festivals where people from a number of communities would get together in the summer for celebrations and trade.

Within a community, the political organization was minimal. Families knew what was needed to provide for their survival and a male family elder often directed the activities of his family. If there was a dispute within the community it would sometimes fall to the male leader of the *kashim* to help reach a solution.

For people of the Arctic, the family unit was more important than was the concept of a tribe. Members of an Inuit family and their dogs are pictured by their camp in Pangnirtung, Northwest Territories (now Nunavut) in this 1951 photograph. *(National Archives of Canada)*

Inuit in Labrador speak a dialect of Inuit-Inupiaq. This painting by Angelica Kauffman, ca. 1786–1772, portrays a woman from Labrador wearing traditional Inuit clothing. *(Library of Congress, Prints and Photographs Division [LC-USZ62-66041])*

Masks were an important part of religious ceremonies for people of the Arctic. An Inuit man wears a ceremonial mask in this 1929 photograph by Edward S. Curtis. *(Library of Congress, Prints and Photographs Division [LC-USZ62-66041])*

Europeans would later turn to the *kashim* leaders as the head of the communities and referred to them as "boss" or "chief." This was more a case of the Europeans trying to impose their idea of government on a people that had little need for that type of political organization.

Scientists have divided the Inuit and Aleut into 22 different groups based on geographical regions. The many Inuit groups have much in common in terms of lifestyle and language. The Aleut and Inuit languages are similar and belong to the language group known as Eskimaleut. The Aleut language has similar roots to the languages of the Inuit but the two split long ago. Among the Inuit, there are two language subgroups—Yup'ik and Inuit-Inupiaq. There are five separate Yup'ik languages that are spoken in Alaska south of Norton Sound and in Siberia.

North and east of Norton Sound, all the way to Greenland, the Inuit people speak a dialect of Inuit-Inupiaq. The dialects vary geographically and people who speak different dialects but live close to each other can understand each other's dialect. The further apart the two Inuit-Inupiaq speakers are located the less likely they are to understand each other.

RELIGION

Most Aleut and Inuit had a similar set of beliefs. Their lives were interwoven with the world of souls and spirits. They believed in the existence of both good and bad spirits.

They tried to conduct themselves in such a way as to avoid the consequences of getting on the bad side of the spirits. Evil spirits were believed to be able to cause both emotional and physical illness if angered. At the same time, if someone offended a good spirit, the outcome of the hunt could be affected.

Because of this, there were many strict rules known as taboos that the people of the Arctic followed. One of the most critical taboos had to do with the separation of land and sea animals. The meat from a seal was never cooked or served with the meat from a land animal like a caribou. During the seal hunting season, the women were not supposed to work on caribou skins. The taboo against mixing land and sea animals even spilled over into clothing. A seal fur parka could not be trimmed with fur from land animals and vice versa. A caribou dress could not include any part of a sea animal. They did this so as not to anger the spirits, who could make it hard for the hunters to be successful.

There was also a hierarchy of spirits. A creator spirit was believed to be above the other spirits. The Sun and Moon were also controlled by separate and powerful spirits. One of the most important spirits that most of the people of the Arctic believe in is Sedna. They believe that Sedna had once been a human who became the spirit in charge of all the sea mammals.

To keep spirits like Sedna happy was one of the important duties of the shamans who live among the people of the Arctic. A shaman is part priest and part healer. The village shaman would know how to deal with wounds and set bones. He or she would also be able to deal with diseases that were caused by problems between the patient and the spirit world.

Traditional Arctic people believe that all living things—

This fish skin frock was typical of what people of the Arctic would wear to protect themselves from the frigid climate. In the cultures of the people of the Arctic it traditionally is forbidden for clothing to contain both sea and land animal skins. (Alaska State Library PCA 20-235)

SEDNA

The story of Sedna varied from region to region throughout the Arctic but the basic facts of the story remain the same. Sedna was a beautiful young woman who lived with her father and refused to get married. Suitor after suitor was rejected by her, until one day a handsome young man who was not known to her village appeared and offered to marry her and share his wealth of food and furs. Finally, Sedna agreed to marry him and her father was happy when she left home with her new husband.

However, Sedna's husband took her to his island where there was no house. When Sedna complained to her husband, he revealed his true being by turning into the trickster Raven. Raven brought Sedna raw fish to eat but did not provide for her in other ways. Sedna sat on the edge of the sea, crying about how foolish she had been to turn down all the good hunters at home and falling for Raven. Far over the sea, her father could hear her cries and came looking for her.

When Sedna's father arrived, she told him about Raven and he agreed to take her home. They left in his kayak and soon saw Raven coming after them. Raven swooped down and stirred the seas around them into a storm. Fearing for his life, Sedna's father pushed his daughter out of his kayak in hopes of appeasing Raven. Sedna refused to go back to her husband and clung to her father's boat.

Afraid that Sedna would upset his kayak, her father hit her hands with the blade of his paddle. He severed her fingers at the first joint. When the pieces of her fingers fell into the sea they became seals. Sedna grabbed the boat again, and her father hit her fingers again. This time, the pieces of her fingers that came off became walruses. The third time this happened, whales were created and without any fingers Sedna sank to the bottom of the sea where she continues to dwell and be responsible for the sea animals that the people depend on.

(Author's note: This version of the Sedna myth was compiled by the author from a variety of sources.)

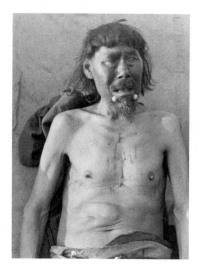

plant, animal, and human—have souls. They also believe that dreams are journeys that their souls take. However, it is possible for a soul to become lost or captured by evil spirits during these journeys. When this happens, the person would become sick and it was up to the shaman to journey to the land of dreams and bring the person's soul back. Shamans also made amulets that were believed to have power to help and protect people.

Left: For people of the Arctic, the shaman was essential for maintaining the health of the community. A shaman from Mackenzie Delta, who has piercings of walrus ivory below his lips, poses for this 1905 photograph. *(Northwest Territories)*

Inuit from various families would cooperate during large tasks, such as preparing for celebrations. In this photograph, a group of Inuit in Point Barrow, Alaska, cut up whale blubber for a feast. *(Library of Congress, Prints and Photographs Division [LC-USZ62-112834])*

TRADE AND COOPERATION

Just as everyone within a family unit had to cooperate to ensure the family's survival, at times the members of an entire village or area joined together for tasks that required intensive labor. This might be after a successful whale hunt when a large whale was brought to the beach to be butchered. Sometimes during the caribou migration, large groups of people would band together to ambush the herds. Also, during the spring spawning runs of fish, groups of people would work together to catch and preserve large quantities of fish for later use.

Although trade became more important after the arrival of Europeans in the Arctic, a certain amount of trade went on prior to that. Most trade among the Inuit took place during summer gatherings. Some of the summer fairs were quite large and served not only as a time of trade but also as a time of social interaction between related villages. It was at these summer fairs that many marriages were arranged. Little trade took place between the Indians of the Subarctic and Arctic as the two groups often considered each other enemies.

3

Houses, Clothes, Tools, and Transportation

HOUSES

Living in the Arctic required a number of types of housing. The traditional type of house a family lived in depended on their location and the time of year. The Aleut tended to live in permanent villages, building rather substantial houses that might house as many as 20 or more people. The houses of the Aleut, barabaras, were usually partially dug down three to four feet into the ground. These houses tended to be oblong or rectangular and were built using a variety of materials.

When possible, the Aleut used driftwood logs as there are no large trees on their islands. When there was not enough wood to build the whole frame of the house, whale bones were also used in its construction. Once the frame of the house was finished, it was covered with skins and then a layer of dried grass. Blocks of sod were cut and these were then laid over the layer of grass. The Aleut entered their houses via a hole in the roof and used notched logs as their ladders.

Inside the Aleut house, there were two or more cubicles along the walls where individual families lived. These areas were covered with fine woven grass mats. Mats were also hung to divide the family space from the common area. The houses were lit with small stone lamps that burned whale oil. Most Aleut did not have open fires in their houses. What little cooking they did could be done over the heat from their lamps.

The Inuit who wintered on land also built houses that were sunk into the ground. They also had to use whatever materials were available to them. Permanent houses often included wood, stone, sod, bone, skins, and even snow. Some houses also had translucent windows made from the thin material of animal guts. Unlike the Aleut, the Inuit did not enter their houses from the roof. Instead there were usually two entrances. If the house was used in the milder months, there might be a ground level door. However, in the winter, going in and out through these doors would cause too much heat to be lost. The winter entrance was usually a tunnel that was as much as six feet below the surface of the ground and up to 20 feet long. The entrance

This photograph shows a barabara, a traditional dwelling for the Aleut that could house up to 20 individuals. Barabaras were often constructed from driftwood or whale bones and then covered with animal skins, mud, and grass. *(Alaska State Library)*

Inuit houses were built from materials that were readily available such as wood, stone, and dirt. Two children stand in the doorway of a dwelling next to grown men Abel (left) and Joshua (right) in this 1886 photograph taken in Hopedale, Newfoundland. *(National Archives of Canada)*

Normally used for temporary housing, igloos were designed for maximum heat retention. In this photograph from 1952, an Inuit family gathers in an igloo in Devon Island, Northwest Territories (now Nunavut). *(National Archives of Canada)*

tunnel often had small dug out areas along the walls that were used for storage. The entrance into the house was usually a hole in the floor. Above the dirt floor, there were raised platforms where people spent most of their time.

This system kept the extreme winter cold from entering the house. It has been reported that inside an Inuit house in the winter, the floor temperature might be right around freezing and food would be left on the floor to keep it cool. At the same time, the temperature on the raised platform where people slept and spent most of their time would be from 60° to over 70° Fahrenheit.

Many Inuit, especially those in central Canada, would spend their winters on the ice where

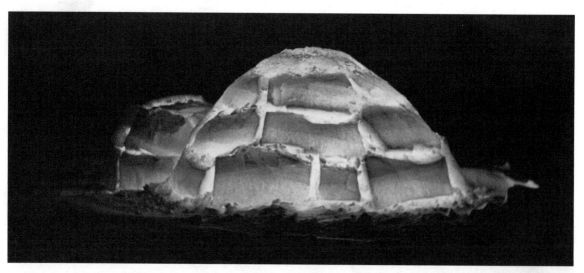

Despite popular conception, igloos were most often built to provide temporary housing for Inuit while they were on hunting expeditions or otherwise away from their home village. This 1964 photograph shows an igloo glowing at nighttime. *(National Archives of Canada)*

BUILDING AN IGLOO
OR SNOW-HOUSE

A hunter who was going to be staying away from his village in the winter could build a small igloo or snow-house in a very short period of time. Temporary igloos were quite small with the top of the dome about five feet high and a diameter of about seven feet. The snow needed to build an igloo had to be of a special type. New, fluffy snow will not hold together when cut in blocks. Windblown snow that has built up into a solid drift works best. When the igloo builder found the right type of snow, he would begin cutting blocks of snow that were approximately six to eight inches thick, two feet high and three to four feet long. The only tool involved was a snow saw or knife that might traditionally be made of bone or wood. Later, European knives and saws were used in igloo making.

Each block had to be cut with special angles. The first row of blocks around the diameter of the igloo was shaped to form a ramp. The igloo was constructed from the inside and the doorway was the last thing that was cut. Each block that was added was cut so that it would lean in, creating the dome. After the dome was finished and the door was cut low in the wall, a small tunnel might be created to protect the entrance from the wind. In some cases, if the igloo was not going to be used for very long, the hunter would just build a snow wall on either side of the doorway to cut the wind.

A group of Inuit works to construct an igloo in Bernard Harbour in this 1915 photograph. Smaller igloos could be constructed in about an hour. *(National Archives of Canada)*

This engraving from 1834 shows a group of igloos and Inuit from Baffin Island in what is now central Nunavut. Igloos were sometimes interconnected by a system of underground tunnels. *(National Archives of Canada)*

they could more easily hunt seals and other marine mammals. When spending extended periods on the ice, the Inuit would build their winter houses out of blocks of snow. Many people are familiar with the smaller dome-shaped Inuit snow-house known as an igloo. Usually the smaller igloo-style houses were built as temporary shelters when people were away from their winter villages while hunting. These small igloos could be built in about an hour and would protect people from the extremes of winter weather.

In the winter villages that were out on the ice, much larger domed and rectangular snow-houses were built. These houses often included a long entry way that might include a number of smaller chambers that were used for storage. Additional snow was sometimes piled over the snow-house to provide even more insulation from the extremely cold outside temperatures. When building snow-houses, the Inuit would sometimes make a block of ice out of freshwater that would serve as a window. Often, if they moved, they would take the ice-block window with them as freshwater was hard to come by. The inside of the main chamber of a snow-house was usually lined with skins that were suspended from anchors that went between the snow blocks. In some communities, the snow-houses were connected by tunnels so that people could visit each other without going outside.

Many people would stay in their snow-houses until the roofs began to drip as the weather became warmer in the spring. Inside the snow-houses, the benches were covered in a thick layer of furs to protect people from the cold below. All people of the Arctic used some sort of lamps that burned either oil or blubber. Their lamps provided light and heat inside their houses. They were also used for cooking. Drying racks were often built over lamps so clothes could be hung up to dry.

During the short summer, many Inuit traveled to temporary sites to fish and hunt. The usual shelters at these camps were some form of tent. Some of the people of the Arctic used a conical tent where skins covered a pole frame. This structure was similar to the tipis of the Plains and other Indians to the south of the Arctic. The more usual Inuit tent was some form of a dome. The frame was made of wood or bone, depending on the resources that were available. All sorts of skins were used for the tents, including caribou, seal, walrus, and even salmon skins. Although most Inuit moved to fish or hunt during the year, the

Lamps served multiple functions: for lighting, for heating food, and for drying clothing. Arnaujumajuq Piungittuq trims a seal oil lamp in this 1950 photograph taken in Pond Inlet, Northwest Territories (now Nunavut). *(National Archives of Canada)*

A dome or conical shape was typical of Inuit construction. An Inuit woman kneels outside a summer skin tent in 1947. *(National Archives and Records Administration)*

Parkas, pants, and boots were customary clothing for most Inuit. A group of Inuit pose in this photograph ca. 1871 to 1907. *(National Archives and Records Administration)*

Snow goggles, which were made from willow twigs or antlers, were essential in diminishing the glare of the sun against the Arctic snow. An Inuit man smiles as he models a pair of snow goggles in this 1933 photograph. *(Northwest Territories)*

places they lived during the year were prescribed by tradition and they did not wander like some nomadic tribes.

CLOTHING

The clothing that traditional people in the Arctic wore was made to protect them from the harsh environment in which they lived. All Arctic people wore clothing made from animal skins. Some groups also used bird skins with the feathers left on for inner garments because of their insulating ability. Although there were a number of regional stylistic differences in clothes and their decoration, the basic outfit of all Arctic people was the same.

The wardrobe generally consisted of two complete layers of clothing. The inner layer was a shirt and pair of pants with the fur facing the body. It was done this way to preserve body heat. In the summer months, the inner clothes were reversed and worn with the fur out. Women's pants often had stocking feet while the men usually wore separate socks. In the winter, a second layer of clothing was worn over the inner clothes. The outer layer was made with the fur out to help repel the wind, snow, and cold that are the almost constant enemies of the people of the Arctic. The outer layer consisted of pants and a parka. Women's outer pants tended to be cut fuller, while men's outer pants had a straight leg.

The parka was in many ways the most critical piece of clothing. Although the Aleut and a couple of other groups wore hats instead of hoods, most Inuit parkas included a head-covering hood. Women's parkas often included an extra large hood to accommodate a child. In old pictures of Inuit women, it looks like there is a child riding in their hood. The child is actually strapped to the woman's back and looks out of the mother's hood. Men's parkas were usually cut straight along the bottom and went to the knee or lower. Women's parkas tended to be longer with a rounded flap hanging down in the front and back.

In addition to the two layers of fur clothing, the Inuit wore waterproof boots. Along with their fur socks, some groups included either a woven grass sock or insole that added extra insulation and helped wick perspiration away from the body. Boots were very important as the foot is often the part of the body most vulnerable to the cold. Some groups made a wide variety of boot styles to be used at different times and under different conditions. Groups that spent much of the winter hunting on the ice often made cleats that fit on the bottom of their boots to give them traction on the slippery ice.

Mittens and gloves were also important. They had to be flexible enough to allow people to grasp weapons and paddles, but warm enough to protect the hand from the cold. Often, two layers of mittens were worn by hunters. The larger, outer mitten provided complete protection from the cold,

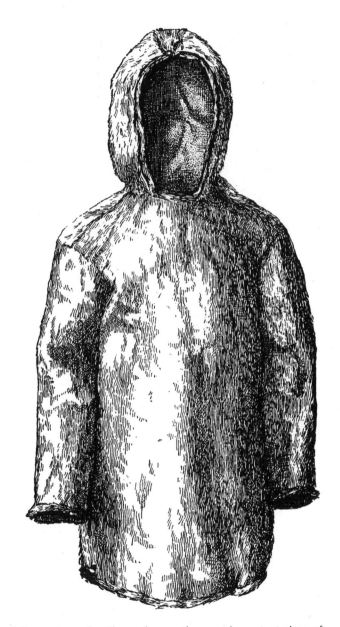

Still popular today, the parka was the most important piece of clothing for the Inuit. Parkas were typically made from caribou, seal, or bird skins. *(U.S. Bureau of Ethnography)*

An Inuit child's outfit includes mittens, which were designed to both warm hands and allow individuals to move their fingers easily. From Nome, Alaska, he poses for this photograph ca. 1900 to 1930. *(Library of Congress)*

while the inner mitten or glove was kept on while performing a task that required dexterity. In addition to their regular double layer of clothes, the people of the Arctic made a number of specialized pieces of clothing.

Ceremonial dress that was extremely ornate was found among most Arctic groups. Special waterproof suits were worn when out in a kayak or when whaling. These waterproof suits were often made from strips of seal or walrus gut that were sewn together to create a suit. Some groups made waterproof parkas that were designed to attach to the opening of a kayak. This kept the hunter dry and also prevented water from getting into the kayak. Other people made one piece waterproof suits that were often worn by whalers. These suits were also made from gut and had an oversized hood that allowed a person to crawl into the suit. A drawstring around the hood was pulled tight once the suit was on.

Clothing was also a sign of wealth. The best hunters showed their success by having a new set of clothes each year. A less successful hunter might have to wear the same clothes for longer periods of time. The quality of a person's clothes also displayed the ability of the women of a family to prepare hides for clothes. Their ability as clothing makers was also on display for all to see.

In addition to clothing, most people of the Arctic decorated their faces with tattoos and piercings. Noses and ears were often pierced as were cheeks and sometimes lips. Tattoos on cheeks and chins were common among some groups on both men and women. Some people also had body tattoos but, considering the fact that their bodies were usually fully covered, body tattoos were not that common. Some mothers wore clothing that was especially baggy so they could carry an infant on their backs under their shirt and/or parka. The shirts were cut loose enough so that the baby could be brought around to the front to nurse without having to be exposed to the cold air.

Facial piercings and tattoos were common for people of the Arctic. An Ugiyaku-Nunivak woman wearing nose and labret piercings poses for this 1929 photograph. *(Library of Congress, Prints and Photographs Division [LC-USZ62-101193])*

TOOLS AND WEAPONS

Traditionally, with the exception of the Copper Inuit who made some tools out of copper, most tools and weapons were made from wood or animal parts and stone. Wood was scarce in most of the Arctic so bone, antlers, and ivory (teeth and tusks) from marine mammals were used for many important items. Men and women had their own tool kits with the items they needed to perform their share of the work.

A woman's tool kit would include numerous tools for butchering animals, preparing hides and food, and making clothes. Each kit would include a variety of blades and scrapers. Some of the scrapers were made of bone, others were made of stone. Probably the most important tool a woman possessed was her ulu. An ulu is a curved blade with a handle in the center of the back of the blade. Traditionally, an ulu was made with a ground slate blade and a handle of wood or ivory. The ulu is still in use, now generally made with modern steel blades. With an ulu, a woman could remove the hide from an animal with

Ulus were essential tools for people of the Arctic. In this 1962 photograph from Kotzebue, Alaska, Anna and Bonnie Thompson use ulus to cut whale meat. *(U.S. Bureau of Ethnography)*

great precision and speed. Various size and style scrapers would then be used to clean any meat and fat from the inner side of the hide. A woman's sewing kit was also an important part of her belongings. Some women were known to have elaborately decorated ivory needle cases. Their sewing needles were made of ivory or bone.

Cooking utensils included a stone oil lamp and many stone bowls for cooking. Meat could be boiled in these bowls, although many meals for Arctic people consisted of raw meat. In addition to her work tools, women would have a number of personal items that included bone or ivory combs as well as a variety of jewelry. Many groups used cradle-boards for their babies. Other women used a sling on their backs to carry their young children.

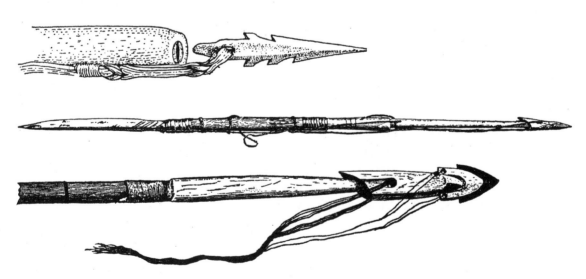

Hunters would select harpoon points based on which animals they were hunting. This drawing depicts harpoon points traditionally used by hunters of the Arctic region. *(U.S. Bureau of Ethnography)*

Men's tool kits consisted primarily of their hunting tools and weapons. Land animals were hunted with a bow and arrows while sea animals were hunted with a variety of spears and harpoons. Each animal from huge whales to small mammals and fish presented the hunter with a unique set of problems. The solution to these problems was a specific set of tools. Like the women's tools, men made their hunting tools from wood, bone, antlers, ivory, and stone. Each hunter made his own tools and weapons. Many tools and weapons were carved with intricate designs that included animals. The Aleut wore special hunting hats that included small carvings of the animals they were hunting. Traditional carvings by Aleut and Inuit carvers are in the collections of many museums. Today, many Arctic people continue to create carvings that are in high demand among art dealers and collectors.

Hunters in the Arctic region typically made their own spears. In this 1935 photograph, Simiguluk, an Inuit from Point Barrow, Alaska, poses with spears he has made. *(National Archives and Records Administration)*

TRANSPORTATION

In the Arctic, there were three main ways to travel—by boat, by foot, and by dogsled. Boats played an important role in the Arctic. The best-known Arctic boat was the kayak and in recent years, this type of boat, made of modern materials, has become extremely popular. Traditional Arctic kayaks were made with a wooden and bone frame and an outer skin of stretched seal or walrus skins. The average kayak was around 18 feet long and had a small opening in the deck for one person. The kayak was propelled with a double-bladed paddle. A paddler could travel a long distance in a short period of time. In rough conditions, paddlers wore a special parka that covered the opening in the deck so that water could not get into the boat.

Kayaks were an important mode of transportation for people of the Arctic and have since become popular for recreation and sport all over the world. A man carries a kayak in this photograph from the early 1900s. *(Library of Congress, Prints and Photographs Division [LC-USZ62-133495])*

Paddlers were very capable and could right their kayaks if they were tipped over in rough water.

Kayaks were used for hunting and fishing. Some larger kayaks held two people. The person in the front carried a spear or harpoon while the paddler piloted the boat near to sea mam-

Capable of holding 10 or more people, umiaks were open boats used by the Inuit for transportation and during whale hunts. Six Inuit surround an umiak in Point Barrow, Alaska, in this 1935 photograph. *(National Archives and Records Administration)*

Dogsleds have been used for transportation for thousands of years. In this photograph from the early 1900s, a man crosses a frozen bay on a dogsled. *(Library of Congress, Prints and Photographs Division [LC-USZ62-132782])*

mals. By the time a young man reached adulthood, he was expected to be able to make his own kayak.

The Aleut only had kayaks. The Inuit had kayaks, but also used a larger, open boat called an umiak. Umiaks could be as long as 30 to 40 feet and were five to six feet wide. A large umiak could carry 10 or more people and up to 1,000 pounds of goods. Like the kayak, the umiak was made with a wooden and whale bone frame and then covered with waterproof skins. Walrus skin was used on many umiaks. An umiak is paddled using single-bladed paddles by a number of people at the same time.

Umiaks were used both for travel and hunting. Whaling was one of the primary uses of an umiak. Whaling trips were led by the owner of the umiak and involved a large group of whalers from a single village. When traveling by umiak, a group camping on shore at night could use their overturned umiaks like tents to provide shelter at night. Kayaks and umiaks were a great way to travel around the many bays and islands of the Arctic coastline in the warmer months, however, in the winter much of that water was frozen over. In the winter, Arctic people had to travel over snow and ice to hunt.

Thousands of years ago, the people of the Arctic domesticated the dog and created the original sled dogs. Teams of dogs were used to pull large sleds over the frozen Arctic land and frozen seascape. In the fall, whole villages would load all their belongings onto their sleds and travel over the ice to their winter homes. Smaller sleds were used by hunters to carry their weapons out onto the ice to hunt seals and then carry the animals they killed back to their village.

Dog sleds, like boats, were usually made out of a composite of wood and bone lashed together with leather straps. Runners were usually made of bone. At times, the runners had water put on them. As the water froze, the coating of ice made the runners as smooth as glass. The frozen runners glided over the snow with practically no friction. Today dog sledding is a popular sport and dog sled teams tend to have pairs of dogs strung out in front of a sled. Traditional dogsledders though tend to have their dogs fanned out in front of them by using different lengths of leads.

In the warm months, when there was little snow or ice, people had to walk. When people moved from fishing camps to hunting camps, they had to carry their belongings. It was not uncommon for sled dogs to wear side packs and help carry their owner's goods. In the winter, generally people also had to walk as their sleds were for carrying goods. The people of the Arctic, like other American Indians, used snowshoes in the winter. They also devised a number of styles of cleats that went over their boots to give them traction on snow and ice.

4

Daily Life in the Arctic

In the more temperate areas of North America, the year can be broken into four distinct seasons; in the Arctic, life is more broken down by just two seasons. Some people live and hunt on the frozen seas from October into May and lakes and ponds start freezing over in September and remain frozen in some locations until June. Winter dominates the calendar with a short break for summer. No matter what time of year it was in the Arctic, the pursuit of food was always the primary activity of most tra- ditional groups prior to European influence. In different parts of the Arctic and at different times of the year, priority was placed on differ- ent animals. Some Inuit, like the Caribou Inuit, lived away from the coast and were extremely depen- dent on caribou. At the same time, the island homes of the Aleut had no large herds of animals and they depended primarily on sea mammals for their subsistence. Over hundreds of generations, the people of the Arctic had developed set patterns to their territories and their movements throughout their ranges during the year.

A caribou stands inside a forest. Caribou has been an important source of food for the Inuit, especially for those who live away from the sea and its source of fish and sea mammals. *(U.S. Fish and Wildlife Service)*

People of the Arctic traditionally traveled during the summer months and set up temporary hunting and fishing camps. Harold Kalluk (left) and Joseph Idlout (right) stand by the corpse of a seal they harpooned in Pond Inlet, Northwest Territories (now Nunavut), in this 1952 photograph. *(National Archives of Canada)*

The wolf dance was an important ritual for the Kaviagamutes of Alaska. A group of wolf dancers, some of whom wear masks, pose for this 1914 photograph. *(Library of Congress, Prints and Photographs Division [LC-USZ62-101282])*

WINTER

Most groups traveled during the summer months to hunting and fishing camps, but by October, they moved to their permanent winter villages. The Aleut stayed in their permanent villages year round. The people of the Arctic had a rich spiritual life that was wrapped around their dependence on hunting. A number of religious festivals were part of Arctic life. The most important of these took place during the winter.

Religious Ceremonies

The primary winter ceremony varied depending on location and the most important animals hunted. In communities where seals were

BLADDER FESTIVAL (THE FEAST FOR SEALS' SOULS)

Among the many winter festivals in the Arctic, the Bladder Festival had some unique elements. The main one is the use of the bladders of seals (in some places walrus and small whale bladders are included). The Inuit believe that the soul of a seal is contained in the animal's bladder. During the year, the bladders of the seals killed by hunters are saved. When the time of the Bladder Festival approaches, the year's bladders are pulled out and inflated with air. The spherical bladders are then painted and hung as decorations in the community's ceremonial house. As the end of the multiday Bladder Festival approaches, the bladders are deflated and taken out through the building's smoke hole. It was believed that the smoke helps transport the souls contained in the bladders.

After the bladders have been removed from the building, a hole is cut in nearby sea ice. The bladders are pushed into the water through the hole in the ice. It is believed that the souls that were contained in the bladders are returned to the sea where they will become new animals. The Inuit believe that when the ceremony is performed properly, new animals will return to the group's hunting grounds and allow themselves to be killed again for the benefit of the people.

the main source of subsistence, the Bladder Festival was the primary ceremony of the year. Among the inland Inuit, the Caribou Festival was most important. In the Alaskan Arctic, they celebrated the Whale Feast. Some groups held what was known as a Messenger Feast.

Although the various winter feasts and festivals had different elements, they all shared a number of aspects. The most important part of all these observances was the idea of renewal. Some of them took place at the time of the winter solstice, the day that marks the halfway point of winter in terms of the Sun. Many of the ceremonies could be compared to a combination of the modern holidays of Christmas and New Year's. Most of the ceremonies involve gift giving and also mark the beginning of the new year.

Another common aspect of the winter ceremonies was the

Traditionally, Inuit would wear new clothing during ceremonies to symbolize renewal. This image from an 1824 engraving depicts Inuit children dancing to the beat of a drum during a ceremony. *(National Archives of Canada)*

Eskimo Dance Masks
St. Michael, Alaska.

When worn by shamans, dance masks added a spiritual element to a ceremony. A postcard from St. Michael, Alaska, from the late 19th or early 20th century displays the various styles of dance masks worn during Inuit ceremonies. *(National Archives and Records Administration)*

wearing of new clothes. The time prior to these ceremonies was usually set aside so that the women of the community could make new clothing for their families. The new clothes would be worn for the following year. During the time the women were finishing the new clothes, the men attended to their hunting weapons. New weapons were made or old ones were repaired for the winter hunting season that followed the ceremonies. Most of the ceremonies were multiday events and some Messenger Feasts might last a few weeks.

All of the ceremonies involve communal feasts and are often followed by a variety of dances and entertainments. Arctic dances are often led by a village's shaman and used to depict his or her spirit visions. Shamans, along with helpers, make elaborate masks that represent characters from the vision. These might include people, animals, and a variety of creatures from the spirit world. After the dances, the masks are buried or burned. Other dances are also performed that are meant solely as entertainment. Singing is also an important part of the ceremonies and men are expected to create new songs in the spirit of renewal.

Traditionally, most of the ceremonies were held by a single village in their ceremonial building. The exceptions were the Messenger Feasts, where one village would host the feast and send messengers out to nearby villages, inviting them to join them. The ceremonial building had a variety of names across the Arctic. In the western areas, it was known as the *kashim* and was also used as a separate living area for the men of the village. In other areas, it was known as the *karigi, qasgiq, qaggi,* or *qashe.* Whatever it was called, it was often the largest structure in a village and was a combination of place of worship and community center. Most groups saw their *karigi,* or whatever they called it, as the place where their world was most closely connected to the spirit world that surrounded them. The smoke hole in the roof of the *karigi* was the point where communication between the two worlds took place. The one message that all Arctic people wanted to make clear to the spirit world was their thanks for the animal spirits that had allowed them to be successful in their hunts. They also asked for continued success in the hunting season that would follow the festival.

Winter Hunting

As the Arctic winter progressed, more and more ice built up in the surrounding seas. Many of the Inuit moved offshore and set up their winter villages out on the ice. It was through and along the edges of the ice that most of their winter hunting took place. Both individual and group hunts took place in the winter. Seals were the primary prey of the winter hunters. In addition to seals, they also hunted walruses and even polar bears.

An Inuit man holds two messenger sticks in this photograph from the early 1900s. The notches on the sticks represented the invitation, and the items attached to the sticks were examples of gifts to bring the host. For a Messenger Feast, a village would send messengers to invite nearby villages to join them in celebration. *(Alaska State Library)*

Common in the Arctic, walruses were hunted by the Inuit and Aleut. The skin, tusks, and meat of the walrus could be used for food, clothing, and tools. *(U.S. Fish and Wildlife Service)*

An individual hunting seals had to have great skill and patience. Seals are able to stay under the ice for 10 to 15 minutes and maintain a number of breathing holes in a given area. The technique was to locate a breathing hole and wait for the seal to come to the surface for air. Often a specially trained dog was used to find the breathing hole. If a group of hunters worked together, they would find a number of holes in a given area and each wait at a different hole. The hunter would have to stand at the hole with his seal spear at the ready as the seals would only surface enough to exhale and inhale through their noses and then submerge again.

The spear that was used when hunting at breathing holes was specially designed for the task and had a special point that was attached to a braided leather line. The point was designed so that it detached from the shaft of the spear and stuck in the animal. When a seal came up to breathe, the hunter would spear the seal in the head and then hold onto the rope until the seal either died from its wound or drowned.

After the seal died, the breathing hole had to be enlarged so that the seal could be dragged up onto the

A polar bear strides across the ice near Barrow, Alaska. Despite their intimidating size, polar bears were targets of hunting by people of the Arctic. *(U.S. Fish and Wildlife Service)*

SEALS

Seals are mammals that have adapted to life in the water. Their primary food is fish. Although seals are found in many oceans of the world and even some large lakes, there are more seals in the cold waters of the Arctic than anywhere else. The most numerous Arctic seal is called the ringed seal in English. In Yup'ik, it is the *niknik,* while in Inupiat it is called the *natchcek.* Traditionally, this was the seal that was most often hunted by the Inuit. The biggest ringed seal reaches five feet in length and weighs as much as 150 pounds.

Ringed seal females give birth in March or April to one seal pup. The pups are white and are usually born in snow dens on the ice. The reason for the dens and the color of the pups is to help protect them from polar bears. Seal pups are the primary food of polar bears. It is believed that older females find better places to den and have a higher success rate in raising their pups. Young and inexperienced females are often found on drift ice where they and their pups are easier prey for polar bears.

A number of other varieties of seals were also hunted. These included the bearded seals that often weigh between 600 and 800 pounds. All parts of the seal were used by the people of the Arctic. The meat and organs were eaten. Oil was extracted from the thick layer of fat that protected seals from the cold Arctic water. The hides were used for kayaks and clothing. The bones were used to make tools and other utensils.

A bearded seal relaxes on the ice. The Inuit used every part of the seals they hunted—for food, lamp oil, kayak material, clothing, and tools and utensils. *(U.S. Fish and Wildlife Service)*

ice. If the hunters were very hungry, they would begin the job of butchering the animal right at the kill site. Otherwise, the hunters would load the seal onto a sled and take it back to the village for the women to butcher.

Once the hunters brought any animals they killed back to their village, it was up to the women to butcher them. The animal was divided up on a very strict basis with the hunter who killed it getting the choicest parts. If it was a group hunt, the other hunters would also get a share. The women would use their special ulu knives to remove all the parts of the animal with care so that nothing was wasted. If there was more than

An Inuit man poses by his dogsled, which is laden with seals he successfully hunted. Seal hunters would often transport seal carcasses to the women of the village, who would prepare the meat for a meal. *(National Archives of Canada)*

Seal hunters would patiently wait for seals to surface for air, after which the hunter would attempt to spear them. A man raises a spear, ready to hunt seal through the hole in the ice he has made in this photograph from the 1930s. *(Northwest Territories)*

could be eaten immediately, it was saved for later use. The most common way to preserve meat, especially in the winter, was to freeze it either in a chamber off the winter house or in a storage pit in the frozen ground. Even in the warmer months, meat could be refrigerated in pits that reached down to the permafrost.

Seal oil was used for heat, light, and some cooking. However, most meat was eaten raw. The oil was one of the Inuit's most valuable commodities. Those who had a surplus could trade it for a number of other goods. Oil was stored in seal skins that had been tanned and then carefully sewn up to be watertight. Some meats were also preserved by packing them in oil.

When people had enough to eat and food stored for the future, they would spend time together. The storytellers of the family would entertain and educate the group. Stories always served a number of purposes. Most stories were entertaining as the storyteller would often act out the various parts of the story. Mixed up in the stories were the history and myths of the group. Some of the stories were also intended to instruct the children in proper behavior. Many of the stories involved the Raven who was one of the major characters in the spirit world of the Arctic.

Toward the end of winter, the ice in the Arctic seas would start to move, creating openings known as leads. This usually sig-

The south slope of Alaska's Brooks Range in summer

The Arctic National Wildlife Refuge of Alaska in winter

Stone lamp, ca. A.D. 1000

Pre-1741 ivory sculpture of a human head from
St. Lawrence Island, Alaska

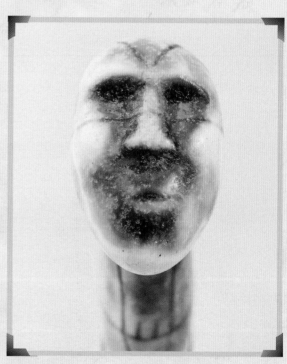

Stone lamp, designed to hold seal or fish oil
for burning

Sculpted ivory drag handle from Point Barrow,
Alaska, pre-1741

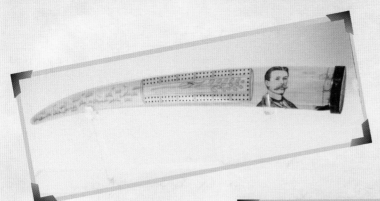

Cribbage board made from walrus ivory, ca. 1900

Masks, made from ivory, wood, thread, and beans, from the Yup'ik of western Alaska

Sewing and hunting accessories made from ivory

Ball made from pieces of dyed or bleached sealskin, stuffed with caribou hair, from St. Lawrence Island, Alaska

Yup'ik fish-mask made from wood and feathers, from western Alaska

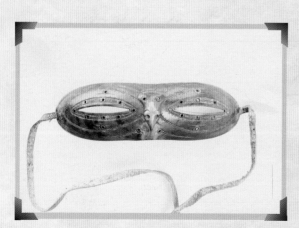

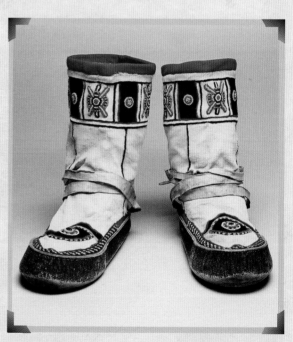

Ivory snow goggles designed to resemble an animal face

Intricately beaded pair of calfskin boots made by Daisy Lane in 1950 in Point Hope, Alaska

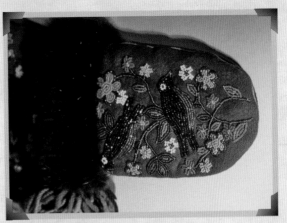

Athabascan mitten made from moosehide, beads, beaver, cotton, satin, and flannel, ca. 1920

Seal gut cape from the Pribilof Islands, Alaska, ca. 1880

Man's summer suit, made from caribou skin, beads, sinew, and cotton

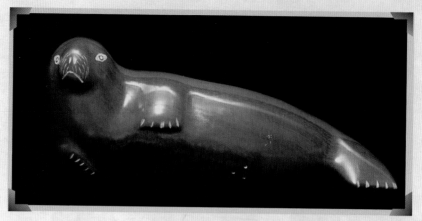

Inuit seal carving by Nina of the Metiq Cooperative, ca. 1960

Inuit walrus carving by Simeonie of the Metiq Cooperative, ca. 1960

Yup'ik mask made from wood, pigment, and feathers, ca. 1900

Late 1800s/early 1900s postcard of an Inuit girl standing on snowshoes and holding a harpoon

ESKIMO GIRL ON SNOW SHOES, ALASKA.

COPYRIGHT 1907 BY CASE & DRAPER.

Inuit man bending down to harness a sled dog in Baker Lake, Northwest Territories (now Nunavut), in 1957

Man carving a traditional igloo in Iaqluit on March 15, 1999, in preparation for a festival celebrating the creation of the territory of Nunavut

Nina Kuppak sledding down a hill in Iqaluit, Canada, on February 27, 1999

Singer-songwriter Susan Aglukark during a performance celebrating the fifth anniversary of the creation of the province of Nunavut, Canada, on April 15, 2004

Performers holding up drums while singing during a ceremony to celebrate the creation of the new territory of Nunavut on April 1, 1999, in Iqaluit

Sealskin containers were used to hold items such as food and oil. Containers made from sealskin are arranged on the ground in this 1929 photograph by Edward S. Curtis. *(Library of Congress, Prints and Photographs Division [LC-USZ62-116541])*

naled the beginning of the whaling season for those Arctic groups who hunted whales. The Aleut did not have umiaks so they would use their kayaks to drive a whale into a shallow bay where waiting hunters could harpoon it and drag it on shore. Other groups went after whales in one or more umiaks.

The leader of the whaling group was known by some groups as the *umialik* by others as the *umelik* and he was often the owner of the umiak. The crew of his boat would usually be made up of male members of his extended family. The umialik would often undergo special ceremonies to prepare himself for the struggle he would face finding and killing a whale.

Everyone in a whaling crew would receive a portion of the whale, but the size of the portion depended upon the prominence of the hunter. Three women work together to cut up a beluga whale in Kotzebue, Alaska, in this 1929 photograph. *(Library of Congress, Prints and Photographs Division, [LC-USZ62-115975])*

The procedure for killing a whale in open water was difficult and dangerous. First, the boat had to be maneuvered close enough to a surfacing whale that a harpoon could be thrown into it. Rather than allow the whale to drag the boat as was done by American and European whalers who came to the Arctic in the 19th century, the Inuit attached floats to the harpoon. The float made it easy to follow the whale and difficult for the whale to dive deep. The floats were made of seal or other animal skins that were sewn up so they would hold air.

The harpooners sometimes used a throwing board, which gave their harpoons more velocity. Often, multiple harpoons were not enough to kill the whale and the boat had to be brought close enough alongside the whale that one of the crew could stab it with a special lance that was designed to penetrate to the whale's vital organs.

Once the whale was dead, it had to be towed back to the solid ice where it could be butchered. On shore, the whale was presented to the wife of the umialik who would oversee the butchering. As in other hunting situations, a whale was divided up according to a traditional order. The hunter who threw the first harpoon would be rewarded with the choicest share. Everyone in the whaling crew would receive a share. If other boats were involved, even if they just helped tow the whale to the butchering site, their crews also received shares. Numerous different types of whales were hunted by the Arctic people. When Europeans began whaling in the Arctic, they would often hire Aleut and Inuit hunters to help them.

SUMMER

Traditionally, some Inuit were able to hunt from the ice into April and even May. As the ice began to break up, it was time to leave the winter villages and head to a number of temporary camps to hunt, fish, and gather berries and other plants. During the summer, different groups of Inuit got together to trade and socialize.

Fishing

As the ice leaves the rivers and lakes of the Arctic in early summer, fish begin their annual migration from the ocean to their freshwater spawning places. At times during these spawning runs, the waters in the rivers are full of fish. Many Arctic groups had one or more traditional fishing locations where they went each summer and set up camp. Some of these camps were used so many times that they built permanent structures there to stay in. At most camps, however, people erected tents to sleep in during the time they were harvesting fish.

Traps such as this one were one of the methods people of the Arctic used in order to catch fish. A man holds a black fish trap in this 1940 photograph. *(Alaska State Library)*

By locating salmon runs, fishermen were able to systematically catch numerous fish. A group of Inuit wades along a stone fish weir while spearing salmon in this photograph taken in the early 1900s. *(Library of Congress, Prints and Photographs Division [LC-USZ62-112765])*

The Arctic people used a wide variety of techniques to catch a number of different fish. Of primary importance were various types of salmon and Arctic char that were plentiful during their summer runs. White fish, northern pike, and a few other varieties were caught in freshwater. In the bays of the Arctic seas, halibut and flounder were regularly caught by some groups. Sometimes, nets woven from animal sinew or grass were used to catch fish. At other times, a bone hook on a line was the preferred method.

During the spawning runs, when there were large numbers of fish in a river, people would stand in the water with special spears and catch large quantities of fish very quickly. The spears had three prongs. The middle prong stuck into the fish while the two side prongs were designed to keep the fish from slipping off the middle point. In some places, people built weirs and used fish traps. A weir in the Arctic was usually made of stone walls erected in a stream or river that forced the fish to swim through narrow gaps. Fish traps made of driftwood or loosely woven baskets were placed in the gaps to catch fish. People with spears could also be positioned at the gaps in the weir to spear fish as they tried to swim past in the narrow openings. In the docu-

NANOOK OF THE NORTH

Nanook of the North is considered by many film historians to be the first documentary film ever made. Director Robert Flaherty, who had spent a number of years in the far north as a surveyor for the Canadian railroad, began taking film footage of the Inuit that he met. The film from his first attempt was lost when Flaherty accidentally set the film on fire with a cigarette. Flaherty decided to try again and persuaded Revillion Frères, a French fur company, to fund the making of the film. Flaherty spent from August 1920 to August 1921 among the Inuit of Quebec along the shore of Hudson Bay filming the life of the man he called Nanook and his family.

Although the film has been criticized by some scholars because Flaherty and Nanook staged a number of the scenes, many others have praised the film for giving the world a glimpse into the lives of the Inuit people. Nanook and his family were engaged in the fur trade but the film tries to portray a more traditional lifestyle. In the movie, there are scenes of igloo building, dog sledding, hunting, kayaking, fishing, and other aspects of Inuit life. On a tragic note, Nanook died during a hunting trip a short time after the film was released. The film had gained such international popularity that Nanook's obituary appeared in newspapers around the world.

mentary film *Nanook of the North,* made in the 1920s, Nanook (the main character in the film) is shown fishing at an opening in the ice. He uses a small lure that does not have a hook to attract salmon close to the surface where he can spear them.

For preservation, fish were either dried in the sun or smoked. At this camp in Itimangnak, fish hang on lines for drying. *(Northwest Territories)*

Food caches, which were constructed with wood and raised on stilts, were commonly used to store dried fish and meat. The raised structure prevented animals from entering and thus protected the food. *(Library of Congress, Prints and Photographs Division [LC-USZ62-107327])*

At the fishing camps throughout the Arctic, many more fish were caught than could be eaten fresh. The Inuit and Aleut had a number of ways to preserve fish to eat later. One of the simplest ways to preserve fish was to dig a pit that reached down into the permafrost (the layer of earth that stayed frozen year round) and then bury the fish in these natural refrigerators. Other fish were dried on racks in the sun and/or over small fires that aided in the drying process. The smoke from the fires contributed to the preservation of the fish as well as adding a flavor. Smoked salmon is still considered a delicacy by many in the Arctic and far beyond.

Often the women of a group were left to do much of the fishing and fish preparation, while the men went hunting. In early summer, and then again after their calves were born, hundreds of thousands of caribou travel between their summer and winter ranges. Caribou hunting was important to almost all Inuit.

Summer Hunting

As with their fishing camps, many Inuit groups had traditional caribou hunting territories. For the Inuit who lived away from the coast, caribou accounted for up to 90 percent of their food. For some coastal groups, caribou hunting was a supplement to their primary hunting of sea mammals. A few coastal groups did not have access to caribou migration routes and would trade for caribou hides as they were an important material for Inuit clothing.

Those who hunted caribou used a number of techniques. When large groups of people were able to work together, caribou drives were preferred. In this technique, a number of cairns (piles of rocks) were built, creating a huge funnel that might stretch a couple of miles across the tundra. The cairns were often decorated with feathers and pieces of fur that would move in the wind and make the cairns appear alive to the caribou. At the end of the funnel some groups would build a corral where the hunters would hide. Other groups would drive the caribou into a lake or river where they were easier to kill.

While the hunters waited, the rest of the group would drive a herd of caribou between the cairns. Afraid of the people and the "rock monsters," the caribou would follow the funnel to the waiting hunters. When a number of caribou reached the hunters, the slaughter began. The hunters would use bows and arrows, spears, and even knives to kill as many caribou as they needed.

At other times, hunters would ambush caribou from their kayaks as they swam across at a river or narrow lake crossing. In many ways, harvesting the caribou was relatively easy as long as they followed their traditional migration routes at the expected time. If, for some reason, the caribou migrated when not expected or did not come to a crossing where Inuit hunters waited, there could be serious consequences for the hunters and their group. When the hunters were successful, there was much work to be done at the hunting camp. Meat had to be removed from the carcasses. Sinew (the tough material surrounding the muscles) had to be dried to be made later into thread and rope. The meat that could not be eaten at the time had to be carefully preserved for later. Meat was also buried in cold storage pits as well as dried and smoked like fish.

The women also had to start the process of tanning the caribou

Inside an igloo, a woman sews clothing made from animal skins. Animal hides from such animals as caribou were often made into clothing. *(Northwest Territories)*

During the summer, people of the Arctic added berries to their standard diet of meat and fish. Two women collect berries in this 1929 photograph taken in Kotzebue, Alaska. *(Library of Congress, Prints and Photographs Division [LC-USZ62-67382])*

hides. Any meat and/or fat had to be carefully scraped from the hides. They were then stretched on racks or staked out on the ground while they were tanned and dried. For the inland Inuit, caribou hides were a valuable trade resource as they were able to later trade with coastal groups for whale and seal oil and ivory.

In some parts of the Arctic, there are large colonies of nesting birds. Where they were available, they were usually hunted. Bows and arrows, spears, and special bird nets on long poles were used to harvest birds. The birds were eaten, and their skins, because of the insulating properties of their feathers, were often used in making clothes. Many Arctic people also gathered eggs from nesting birds in their territories.

Gathering

Meat and fish made up most of the traditional diet of the Arctic people. During the short summer, however, they did gather a number of berries, roots, and edible plants. Cranberries, blueberries, and a number of other berries grow in the nearly endless sun of the short Arctic summers. In addition, a variety of other tundra plants and roots were harvested for food. A variety of grasses were collected by some groups to be woven into ropes and baskets.

Women and children did most of the gathering, and the women preserved the gathered fruit in a number of ways. Some berries were dried whole or pressed into a sheet that was then dried. Other berries were put in large wooden containers and then covered with oil to preserve them. Root plants were stored in clay-lined pits where they would stay edible throughout the winter.

The Summer Fair

One of the highlights of the summer for many Arctic people were the annual fairs that were held in many places throughout the North. These fairs served a number

Drumming was an important part of dances and weddings at fairs for people of the Arctic. A man plays a large hand-held drum, which is made of walrus stomach or bladder, in this 1929 photograph by Edward S. Curtis. *(Library of Congress, Prints and Photographs Division [LC-USZ62-46887])*

of social and economic functions. The main focus of the fair was trade. The surpluses of one group could often be traded to fill the shortages of another group. Oil from seals and other marine mammals, sealed into animal skin bags called pokes, was one of the most sought-after trade goods. Those who had oil to trade were able to barter for anything they might need. Oil was critical in the Arctic where wood and other fuels for heat, cooking, and light were scarce or nonexistent.

In addition to trade, the fairs were also a social gathering. Weddings were arranged and relatives were given the opportunity to visit family members they might not see at any other time of the year. The largest fair at the beginning of the historic period was held at Sheshalik on Kotzebue Sound in Alaska. As many as 2,000 Inuit attended this fair, including people from islands in the Bering Sea and as far away as the Siberian mainland. The fair would last for two or three weeks.

The fairs were also a time of entertainment for people who spent most of their year struggling to survive. Dances were held. Stories were told or performed. Games were played. The Inuit played a number of games, many of which came about as part of their hunting culture. Others, it seemed, were just for fun.

Blanket tosses were a popular game during fairs among people of the Arctic. In this photograph from the late 19th or early 20th century, a woman is bounced in a blanket toss during a spring whaling celebration. *(Alaska State Library)*

Some of the hunting-related games were archery competitions and footraces.

One of the best-known Arctic games is the blanket toss, where a group of people holds a blanket with a person on it and then tosses the person in the air. Some have suggested that the blanket tosses was originally done by hunting parties that were trying to spot game over the rolling plains and miles of ice that make up the Arctic landscape. Another game that was played for fun involved a leather ball that was kicked. The game was very similar to soccer but did not include goal posts.

5

The Coming of the Europeans

The traditional lifestyle of the Arctic existed with little or no European influence much longer than in other culture areas in North America. The harsh climate and difficulty reaching the region isolated the people of the region. Some groups remained completely isolated from contact until the early part of the 20th century. Others, like the Aleut and the Inuit of western Alaska, entered into the fur trade and whaling industry with Russians beginning in the 18th century. During the 18th century, Danes returned to Greenland. They first came in hopes of finding the remnants of the earlier Norse colonies. They stayed to try to convert the Inuit of Greenland to Christianity and to trade for furs and other marine mammal products. In the Canadian Arctic, the Hudson's Bay Company was granted a charter in 1670 that gave it the exclusive rights to trade in the entire Hudson Bay watershed.

RUPERT'S LAND

Some parts of Arctic Canada were the last to be reached by Europeans. However, some of the first Europeans in the American Arctic were explorers looking for a way to get around North America and sail on to Asia. Many believed that a Northwest Passage existed and expeditions were funded to find it. The first was led by English naval captain, Martin Frobisher. In 1576, Frobisher sailed into what would become the Canadian Arctic in search of the Northwest Passage.

Frobisher sailed into the Labrador Sea, between Labrador and Greenland, and continued north to what is now called

An engraving depicts English naval captain Martin Frobisher. Frobisher and his crew attempted to find a Northwest Passage in 1576. *(Library of Congress, Prints and Photographs Division [LC-USZ62-38672])*

Baffin Island. He sailed 150 miles into a large bay that now bears his name, and thought he had found the Northwest Passage. At this time, he made contact with the local Inuit. The drawings and writings done by Frobisher and his crew were some of the earliest accounts of Inuit dress and customs.

The first meeting between the explorers and the Inuit did not go well as the Inuit were hostile and tried to keep Frobisher and some of his crew from landing. Some have suggested that earlier contacts with European fishermen, who had been coming to the cod-rich waters off North America since before the voyages of Christopher Columbus, had already made the Inuit leery of Europeans. Frobisher captured three Inuit and took them back to England. At the same time, five of his men were captured by the Inuit.

Other explorers followed Frobisher. John Davis led expeditions to the same area during the summers of 1585 and 1586. Davis explored further north and discovered the passage between Baffin Island and Greenland that is now called Davis Strait. Famed English explorer Henry Hudson also looked for the Northwest Passage and died in 1611 after being abandoned by his mutinous crew in the bay that now bears his name. A number of others followed Hudson's route into the Arctic and Hudson Bay. The furs they brought back led to the founding of the Hudson's Bay Company in 1670.

King Charles II of England granted a charter in 1670 to his German cousin Prince Rupert and his business associates, giving them the exclusive rights to trade, explore, and exploit all the lands that drained into Hudson Bay. Their company would

THE NORTHWEST PASSAGE

In the 15th century, trade with Asia became important for Europeans. However, the land route through the Middle East was extremely dangerous. Portuguese sailors had found a sea route to Asia by sailing around Africa. Christopher Columbus, an Italian sailing for Spain, was convinced that Asia could be reached by sailing west from Europe. His voyages began the ultimate conquest of the Americas by Europeans. Many believed they could sail around the American continents. Ferdinand Magellan discovered in 1520 that it was possible to sail around the southern tip of South America.

Many tried but failed, often tragically, to find a passage around the northern shore of North America. For thousands of years, the Inuit had lived along the shores of the Arctic Ocean and navigated the waters that were part of a northwest passage. Norwegian Roald Amundsen proved the existence of a passage when he took three years, from 1903 to 1906, to navigate across the Arctic Ocean. In 1969, a specially designed oil tanker/ice breaker, the *Manhattan*, became the first large modern ship to go from Alaska to the Atlantic. It was hoped that the ship would be able to make regular trips carrying oil from the Alaskan North Slope to the east coast of North America. However, the ship was so severely damaged as it forced its way through the ice that the idea of safely shipping oil through the Northwest Passage was abandoned. Recent warming of the Arctic climate has created periods when the Northwest Passage is ice free. Some suggest that if the warming trend continues, ships will be able to regularly travel the Northwest Passage.

have a devastating effect on the Inuit of the region that the Europeans called Rupert's Land.

The Hudson's Bay Company, which still exists today, set up trading posts where they offered European goods in exchange for furs. The American Indians in the English colonies to the south were overrun by colonists who spread disease and war until they were forced to abandon much of the land they had inhabited. In the Arctic, Hudson's Bay Company exploited the Inuit in a different way with almost equally disastrous results.

By introducing European products—especially modern weapons, metal utensils, and cloth—they disrupted the usual subsistence

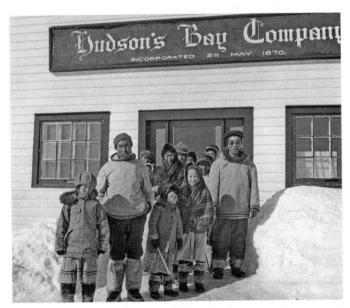

The Hudson's Bay Company, which still exists, served as a base where individuals could trade animal furs for European goods. A group of Inuit from Great Whale, Québec, Canada, poses in front of a Hudson's Bay Company store in this 1946 photograph. *(National Archives of Canada)*

A company trader holds white fox furs that he is attempting to buy from an Inuit man at a Revillon Frères post in the early 1900s. Because of the lucrative nature of the fur trade, Inuit hunters turned their sights on fur-bearing animals and away from the animals they traditionally hunted. *(Library of Congress, Prints and Photographs Division [LC-USZ62-112764])*

practices of the Inuit they met. Inuit hunters began to spend more time pursuing furbearing animals like the Arctic fox, mink, and beaver to trade with the Europeans rather than the traditional animals that provided most of their food. The traders who worked for the Hudson's Bay Company also brought disease to the north.

Epidemics plagued the Arctic. A 1781 smallpox epidemic was reported to have killed nine out of 10 of the people who traded with the company at Churchill. Churchill is located on the western shore of Hudson Bay and could be reached by the Caribou Inuit, as well as the Chipewyan and Cree of the Subarctic Culture Area. By the end of the 18th century, England had taken Canada from the French and had established its control of the north from Labrador to Alaska. In the 19th century, traders would continue to make inroads into the Arctic. They would disrupt traditional ways of life and settlement.

THE RETURN OF THE VIKINGS

In the 18th century, the Vikings who had settled in Greenland hundreds of years ago were considered part-myth, part-history by many in Europe. However, Denmark and Norway, which were ruled by one monarch, still claimed the land. Some even believed that the descendants of those Viking settlements could still be found in Greenland. Early in the 18th century, whalers from other European countries were sailing the waters around Green-

EUROPEAN DISEASE

When the ancient relatives of the Inuit and Aleut left Asia for North America, they became isolated from European and Asian diseases. They therefore had no resistance to diseases such as measles, mumps, and influenza, which Europeans carried and were generally able to survive. The Inuit and Aleut were also exposed to smallpox, which was a deadly disease even in Europe.

Epidemics of these European diseases killed many more American Indians and Alaska Natives than all the wars between Indians and whites. Some estimate that 90 percent or more of the Indian population that existed in the Americas in the 15th century was destroyed by European diseases.

land. The Dutch had gone as far as establishing trade with the Inuit of Greenland.

Many Scandinavians had rejected the Catholic faith and had become members of the Protestant Church started by Martin Luther. It was in part because the king, Frederick IV, decided he had a responsibility to take the "true" religion to any European descendants in Greenland that a missionary expedition was outfitted to go to Greenland. A Lutheran minister named Hans Egede led the expedition in 1721 and set up his first mission at Gothåb.

When he learned that there were no longer any descendants of the Norse settlers in Greenland, Egede decided he should try to convert the Inuit to Christianity. Progress was slow for the mission as they spent their first year building their settlement. It then took Egede a long time to learn the Inuit language so he could spread his message. As

A 1674 engraving depicts Inuit of Greenland wearing fur outfits. Europeans who traded with Inuit from Greenland soon adopted such fashion. *(National Archives of Canada)*

Gesturing to the sky, a Moravian missionary preaches to a group of Inuit in this 1819 watercolor. Lutheran and Moravian missionaries attempted to convert the Inuit to their religions. *(National Archives of Canada)*

Egede went about his missionary efforts, others who came with him began trading with the Inuit.

The Scandinavians who set up the trading posts in Greenland encouraged the Inuit to continue their traditional patterns of hunting and settlement. However, the demand for seal furs and the impact of firearms and European nets used to catch seals upset the balance between the Inuit and their environment. The items that became in demand by the Inuit included firearms and metal tools, as well as tobacco, coffee, and alcohol. The last three items provided no benefits and had a negative impact on the health of the Inuit.

The missionary efforts begun by Egede continued as each trading post soon had a mission. By the 1780s, most of the Inuit along the west coast of Greenland had been baptized in either the Lutheran or Moravian Church. The Moravians were a German Protestant sect that appealed to many Inuit because of their practical approach to Christianity. By this time, there were a number of problems in Greenland.

A number of Inuit, especially women and children, had moved into the communities that grew up around the trading post/missions. Many of these women married Europeans and their children ended up in a kind of limbo. The children of these mixed marriages were considered Greenlanders but did not learn the traditional way of life. They could not contribute to the hunting/trading economy that had developed between the Inuit and Europeans.

On April 19, 1782, a set of new regulations were established to address many of the problems that the presence of Europeans had caused in Greenland. The rules were known as the Instruction of 1782. They called for all children of Greenland, legitimate or illegitimate, Inuit or of mixed marriages, to be raised as "Greenlanders." The sale of alcohol was banned. The traders were told not to trade for food and other necessities that the Inuit needed to survive.

The Instruction also called for a check on weights and measures that the traders used to ensure that they were not cheating the Inuit. There were even conservation parts to the rules. There was a high demand for down from eider ducks and many Inuit had turned their efforts to killing the ducks for their downy feathers that were used to fill quilts, mattresses, and pillows in Europe. The Instruction of 1782 provided rules to prevent illegal trade of down to English whalers who frequented the waters off Greenland in the summer, as well as trying to preserve the eider ducks by limiting the amount of down collected.

One unique aspect of the Instruction was the establishment of a relief fund for the Greenland Inuit who traded with the Europeans. Fines that were imposed on traders who broke the rules of the Instruction, as well as profits from local whaling, were set aside to aid the Inuit when there were times of need. As the 18th century came to an end, there was hope that the Inuit of Greenland would be treated fairly by the Europeans who lived among them.

Peter the Great was the emperor of Russia from 1696 until 1725. He was responsible for sending Russians to explore and claim what is now Alaska. *(Library of Congress, Prints and Photographs Division [LC-USZ62-121999])*

RUSSIANS IN ALASKA

For hundreds of years, Russia had been the source of many of the furs that were sold in Europe as well as those used by the Russians. As Russian fur hunters and traders expanded their territory east across Siberia, they finally reached the Pacific Ocean in the middle of the 17th century. In 1648, a group of traders crossed what would later be called the Bering Straits and arrived on the Alaska coast. The Russians did nothing about the realization that North America was so close to Russia for a long period of time.

In 1728, the Russian czar Peter the Great thought that a Russian presence in North America would be worth pursuing. He chose a Danish sailor serving in the Russian navy, Vitus Bering, to explore the region and establish a Russian claim in North America. Based on Bering's first expedition in 1728 and his second in 1741, Russia claimed what would become Alaska. Bering died in the winter of 1741–42 on the island that now bears his name. However, the survivors of that expedition reported back to Saint Petersburg and fur traders soon followed them into what is now called the Bering Sea.

Many of the fur merchants sent out ruthless groups of armed hunters who soon came into conflict with the Aleut. The Aleut resented the foreigners who were invading their hunting territory. Fighting often resulted between the two groups. However, the Russians brought with them guns and disease, neither of which the Aleut were equipped to resist.

By the time the Russians worked their way across the Aleutian Island chain and reached Kodiak Island in 1762,

COMPETITION FOR ALASKA

The Russians were not the only European power that was interested in Alaska. The Spanish moved north from modern-day Mexico into what is now California, in part to prevent the Russians from coming south from Alaska. They also sent a number of expeditions to Alaska between 1774 and 1790.

Britain, France, and the newly independent United States also took an interest in Alaska. In 1778, one of England's most famous explorers,

Captain George Vancouver sailed from England to what is now Alaska in 1708. Vancouver laid claim to the west coast of Canada for England. The largest city in British Columbia and an island off its coast were subsequently named for him. *(Alaska State Library)*

Captain James Cook was a prominent English explorer who sailed to Alaska in 1778. The British were among many who took an interest in what would later become Alaska. *(Alaska State Library)*

Captain James Cook sailed to Alaska and mapped much of its coastline as well as the Aleutian Islands. His crew acquired a number of sea otter furs, which they sold for amazingly high prices when they reached China. Cook was followed by Captain George Vancouver in 1798. Vancouver's voyage solidified the English claim to the west coast of Canada, which would become the province of British Columbia. The French also made at least one voyage to Alaska, but the French Revolution in 1789 ended their imperial interests.

In this illustration, an Aleut man (left) trades a fur pelt with a Russian man (right). Trade often caused conflict between the Russians and the Aleut. *(Alaska State Library)*

the Aleut population, which has been estimated at as many as 20,000 people, had been reduced by 80 percent. Within less than 100 years, the Aleut population was reduced to fewer than 1,500 people. The Russians had also decimated the otter population of the islands. Toward the end of the 18th century, the Russians turned their attention to the mainland of Alaska and became better organized in their efforts to expand their fur trade in North America.

In 1784, a group sponsored by the company that would later be known as the Russian American Company fought a battle with a group of Inuit on Kodiak Island. After defeating the Inuit, the Russians established a trading fort at Three Saints Bay on Kodiak Island. They would later move to the other side of the island and establish the town of Kodiak. From Kodiak, the Russian American Company spread out along the coast and islands of Alaska using force whenever they found resistance from the Inuit to their north, the Aleut to the west, and Tlingit and other coastal groups to their south.

6

The Aleut and Inuit in the Nineteenth Century

The 19th century was a time of change for many of the Native people of the Arctic. The Russians continued to expand their fur trading enterprises in Alaska. The Hudson's Bay Company did the same in Northern Canada. At the same time, there were two new sets of arrivals in the Arctic. Whalers from Europe and North America pushed further and further into Inuit territory in both the eastern and western Arctic. They often had a negative impact on traditional Inuit culture. The whalers brought new technologies and disease with them while they greatly depleted the whale population of the Arctic. In addition, missionaries from numerous Christian denominations felt they needed to convert the people of the Arctic to their beliefs. In Alaska, by the end of the 19th century, the start of a commercial fisheries industry would also greatly impact the Aleut and Inuit.

MISSIONARIES
The return of Europeans to Greenland in the 18th century was fueled by the missionary desires of Hans Egede and others like him. By the end of the 18th century, their mission had had great success, but it did not last long. In the early years of the 19th century, Denmark chose to become an ally of Napoleon, the self-appointed emperor of France. By the end of the Napoleonic Wars, Denmark had lost Norway and experienced a severe economic crisis. The Danes were forced to cut the budget for the Greenland missions in half. There was also a

As Russia became more interested in what would later become Alaska, missionaries from the Russian Orthodox Church began to convert Aleut to their religion. Holy Ascension Russian Orthodox Church, shown here, was built in 1882 on Unalaska Island in the Aleutian Islands off the coast of Alaska. *(Library of Congress, Prints and Photographs Division)*

lack of resources to support the trade with Greenland. Many Greenland Inuit who had come to depend on the missionaries and traders suffered at this time.

While the Danes were forced to reduce their missionary activities in Greenland, missionaries in Canada and Alaska followed the traders as they moved deeper into Inuit territory. In Alaska, in the beginning of the 19th century, the Russian traders were followed by missionaries from the Russian Orthodox Church. However, in the first half of the century, the Russian missionaries concentrated their efforts in southwestern and southeastern Alaska. In these areas, many Indians and Alaskan Natives are still members of the Russian Orthodox Church. However, it was not until the United States bought Alaska that missionaries penetrated into northwestern and northern Alaska.

When Alaska became part of the United States, a number of American church groups sent missionaries to Alaska. Many of them ended up in the Arctic as the Aleut and southeast Indians remained loyal to the Orthodox Church. Congregationalist, Episcopal, and Presbyterian missionaries arrived in the north by the end of the 19th century. Many of these missionaries had a great impact on the Inuit communities they settled in. The missionaries set up schools and often provided medical services in addition to trying to convert the Inuit. Many of the Inuit, at least on the surface, seemed to accept the ideas of Christianity.

SEWARD'S FOLLY

In 1843, U.S. secretary of state William Marcy first brought up the idea of the United States buying Alaska when he asked the Russian ambassador, Baron Eduard Stoeckl, in Washington, D.C., if it was for sale. At the time, the Russians had no interest in selling their colony in North America. In 1844, the charter of the Russian American Company was extended for another 20 years.

After the American Civil War, the situation in Russian had changed. The Russians had lost a very expensive war against France and Great Britain known as the Crimean War and could not afford to continue to support their Alaskan colony. Baron Soeckl was still the Russian ambassador in Washington and he approached the current secretary of state, William Seward, about buying Alaska. On March 11, 1867, Soeckl and Seward entered into negotiations for the United States to buy Alaska. By the end of the month, the two men had drawn up what is called the Treaty of Cession, which outlined the transfer of Alaska to the United States.

The treaty called for the United States to pay Russia $7.2 million for what some newspapers called Seward's Folly. Little was known about Alaska at the time and some thought buying it was a waste of money. However, Seward convinced the Senate that buying Alaska was in the best interest of the United States. The Senate voted 37 to 2 to approve the treaty. A year later, on July 18, 1868, the House of Representatives appropriated the money for the purchase and Alaska became part of the United States.

This painting depicts Russian and American representatives during the signing of the Treaty of Cession on March 30, 1867. The treaty transferred ownership of Alaska from Russia to the United States for the price of $7.2 million. *(Alaska State Library)*

Almost everywhere the Hudson's Bay Company set up a trading post, and in some places they did not, Catholic and Anglican missionaries tried to bring Christianity to the Inuit of Canada. Some see the influence of the missionaries as serving as a buffer between the Inuit and the negative impact of the traders and whalers in the eastern Arctic. Despite the fact that missionaries might have warned of the hazards of alcohol and other ills of white society, they were still agents of change. They wanted the Inuit to give up their traditional beliefs for Christianity and opposed many of their traditional social practices.

Whether in Canada, Alaska, or Greenland, the influence of missionaries was ultimately disruptive of the traditional life of the Inuit and Aleut. People were encouraged to give up their traditional beliefs. Schools took children away from their families and many children failed to learn the traditional skills that had helped the Aleut and Inuit survive for thousands of years in balance with their harsh environment. Even more upsetting to the balance of Arctic life was the continuation and expansion of the fur trade and the arrival of European and American whalers in the waters of the Arctic.

In this early 1900s photograph, Inuit children sew and knit during a class. Missionaries and schools attempted to assimilate Inuit and Aleut children into non-Native society—often by teaching the children that their traditions were wrong. *(Library of Congress, Prints and Photographs Division)*

BLUBBER, BALEEN, AND THE BOWHEAD WHALE

Starting in the 19th century, two whale products became very valuable. Whale oil, which was made by rendering the fat or blubber of a whale, was used for lights and as a lubricant. To render the blubber into oil, the blubber was placed in huge iron kettles on the deck of a ship where it was heated. As the blubber was heated, the fat was reduced to oil.

Baleen was also sought after. It is the long flexible plates that are found in the mouths of whales that feed primarily on krill—a small shrimp-like crustacean that is plentiful in Arctic waters in the summer. The baleen plates act like filters, catching the krill and allowing the water that is sucked into the whale's mouth to escape. Baleen is very similar to modern-day plastic and was used for a variety of products ranging from the stays in women's corsets to buttons and combs.

The bowhead whale, which is also known as the right whale or Arctic whale, was the most common of the baleen whales. An adult bowhead is between 45 and 60 feet in length and could weigh as much as 200,000 pounds. An adult bowhead has up to 600 baleen plates in its mouth and each plate can be 10 feet long. During the second half of the 19th century, the bowhead whale was hunted almost to extinction. In 1935, an international agreement stopped the commercial hunting of bowheads. Today, there are approximately 5,000 bowhead whales in the world. It is still considered an endangered species that is gaining slowly in numbers and still faces numerous challenges due to human interference in its environment and global climatic changes.

WHALING

Many of the Inuit in northern Alaska and the western Arctic of Canada had little or no contact with whites until whaling ships entered the Arctic waters in the 19th century. In many ways, the whalers had a terrible impact on the people of the Arctic. The men on the whaling ships did not have the lofty ideals that missionaries claimed. Nor were they all that interested in establishing long-term trade arrangements. Their motives were to find and kill as many whales as they could during the short summer season.

The whalers introduced more of the Inuit to European and American goods. They also recruited a number of Inuit to help them in their whaling activities. As time went on and whales became harder to find, the whalers penetrated farther and farther into the Arctic. It soon became necessary for them to spend winters in the Arctic as they could not get to the areas they were hunting in and return in one short summer season.

When whalers started wintering in the Arctic, their impact on the Inuit became even greater. They introduced a number of diseases to the Inuit communities they wintered near. There were also conflicts between the whalers and the Inuit as the whalers tried to find female companions among the Inuit women. Many of the whaling ships that made return trips to the Arctic brought trade goods with them to supplement their income from whaling.

Although all of these changes adversely affected the Inuit, the greatest impact of the whalers was the near destruction of the bowhead and the other baleen whale population in the Arctic. Many Inuit groups had depended on whaling for their subsistence. With the whales all but gone, pressure was put on other food sources. Also, the desire for additional trade goods turned many from subsistence hunting to market hunting for furs and other marketable animal products like walrus ivory. As the rest of the world turned to petroleum for fuel and lubricants, the whales had been almost wiped out, and the life of the Inuit in the far north had been changed forever.

FUR TRADE

The fur trade that had begun in the Russian Arctic and stretched across the north to Greenland in the 18th century expanded even further in the 19th century. The introduction of firearms

After its beginnings in the 18th century, the North American fur trade expanded in the 19th and 20th centuries to encompass an area extending from Alaska in the west to Greenland in the east. A fur dealer poses by some bundles of fur pelts in this photograph taken between 1900 and 1930. *(Library of Congress, Prints and Photographs Division)*

The introduction of rifles to Inuit and Aleut hunters dramatically and permanently altered the practice of hunting and, subsequently, the ecosystem of the Arctic. In this 1915 photograph, a hunter stands by the carcass of a seal he has just killed. *(National Archives of Canada)*

and metal traps into the Arctic increased the efficiency of Inuit and Aleut hunters. The sea otter population of the Aleutians had already been depleted by the beginning of the 19th century. As the 19th century progressed, the fur trade continued to disrupt the traditional lifestyle of the Inuit.

The Inuit had always had a deep respect for the animals they killed and had used as much of the animal as possible. As more and more Inuit turned to hunting specifically for furs to trade, this changed. With modern cartridge rifles that made their way into the Arctic in the second half of the 19th century, Inuit hunters could kill sleeping seals and walruses at longer distances and in much greater numbers. The traditional method of hunting seals at breathing holes was abandoned by many. They found it much easier to hunt sea mammals resting on the ice. With a simple white shield to camouflage them, Inuit hunters could shoot seals and walruses without being detected. Soon the Inuit hunters were killing animals just for the furs and leaving the carcasses. They started trapping animals that had little or no value as food but had valuable fur such as foxes, mink, and beaver.

FUR EXCHANGE RATES

When the Hudson's Bay Company received its charter in 1670, beaver furs were in the greatest demand. A "made beaver" was the term used for the highest quality beaver pelts. Beaver pelts were used primarily to produce felt for hats and other garments. To make felt, the fur of the beaver pelt was scraped off, then pressed together to form a thick cloth that could be easily shaped into hats. During the long period that the Hudson's Bay Company was in the fur trading business, it used the made beaver as the basis for its rate of exchange.

It became the custom for individual trading posts to issue tokens made of shell, bone, wood, or metal that were used like money by the Inuit. The tokens' values were in terms of made beaver pelts. In the 1860s, the company formalized this practice by having a series of coins made. The largest brass coin was equal to one made beaver. Smaller coins were also struck that equaled one half, one quarter, and one eighth of a made beaver pelt. Goods were valued based on how many made beaver they were worth. Furs of lesser value were also bought according to their worth in made beaver pelts.

An Inuit man and woman pose with a dog on a leash in this 1826 illustration. The man on the left wears coins around his neck whose value corresponded to portions of beaver pelts. (*National Archives of Canada*)

Firearms also drastically changed caribou hunting. Caribou hides were one of many furs that the traders wanted. With rifles instead of traditional weapons, the Inuit and the hunters of the Subarctic area where the caribou migrated, soon decimated the caribou herds. At the beginning of the 19th century, there had been millions of caribou that summered in the Arctic. By the middle of the 20th century, estimates put the total number of caribou in Canada below 200,000 animals.

By the end of the 19th century, the demand for fur, especially beaver, had decreased. Fashions had changed and other materials replaced fur. Huge reductions in the numbers of furbearing animals also complicated life for the Inuit. Many found it hard to continue their modified lifestyle as hunters and were forced to settle around trading posts and whaling

The establishment of a commercial fishing industry in Alaska in the 1880s led to the seasonal employment of numerous Inuit and Aleut. Hoonah Cannery of Hoonah, Alaska, is pictured in this 1917 photograph. *(Alaska State Library)*

stations where they could find wage-paying jobs. Most of these jobs, when they could be had, were low paying and seasonal. In Alaska, the commercial fishing industry started up in the 1880s and many Inuit and Aleut found seasonal employment on the fishing boats and in the canneries.

COMMERCIAL FISHERIES

With the whales all but gone and many of the furbearing animals reduced to levels that made hunting them impractical, people who wanted to exploit the wealth of Alaska and other parts of the Arctic turned to fishing. In the 1880s, salmon were still extremely plentiful in the waters off Alaska. This

A caribou grazes against a backdrop of mountains in the Arctic region. The hunting of caribou with firearms has decreased the population from several million in the 19th century to the current estimate of 200,000. *(U.S. Fish and Wildlife Service)*

A prospector crouches while panning for gold in a stream in Alaska. The discovery of gold in the Yukon Territory of Canada on August 17, 1896, encouraged many to travel to the site of the find in hopes of making a fortune. *(Alaska State Library)*

was especially true in the Bristol Bay area in the southeast corner of the Bering Sea.

Although the majority of the boats and most of the profits went to white individuals and companies, many Inuit from around western Alaska began working in the fishing industry. Many of these people worked in the canneries along the coast. Some of the Inuit moved permanently to the fishing centers. Others tried to incorporate working for wages during the summer with a more traditional lifestyle in the winter. The Inuit who did this would move for the fishing season and then return to their ancestral territories when the fishing boats had sailed away and the canneries had shut down for the winter.

The wages earned in the summer were used to purchase items, like guns and cloth, that the Inuit could not manufacture themselves. Many Inuit who moved to the fishing centers lost contact with their traditions and customs. Within a generation or two, these people became completely dependent on the growing white economy of Alaska. Fishing is still an important activity in Alaska and elsewhere in the Arctic. Modern Inuit and other Alaskan Natives have gained control of the fishing industry in their area. They have bought their own boats and canneries, using the resources acquired from various settlements with the U.S. government.

In Greenland, fishing continues to be an important activity as well. Much of the packaged fish consumed in Denmark comes from Greenland. Today, many Greenlanders of Inuit descent are involved in fishing. In the Canadian Arctic, the problems created by the short ice-free season have prevented the growth of commercial fishing in that area.

In this photograph, a crowd assembles in the town of Nome, Alaska. The gold rush was instrumental in creating a population boom in such places as Nome and the Yukon Territory of Canada. *(Alaska State Library)*

GOLD RUSH

The first discovery of gold by whites in the north came on August 17, 1896, on Bonanza Creek, a tributary of the Klondike River in the Yukon Territory of Canada. This was not an area inhabited by Inuit. However, the fastest way to get to the Klondike area was to take a ship up the west coast of North America to Alaska and then travel up the Yukon River to Dawson, Yukon Territory. This route took many prospectors through Inuit territory.

Dawson is located at the point where the Klondike River joins the Yukon River. Within two years, Dawson became a boomtown of 30,000 people. Some Inuit served as guides and packers for the Klondike Gold Rush. When gold was discovered in 1898 in Anvil Creek on the Seward Peninsula of Alaska, Nome became the next big boomtown. By 1900, 20,000 prospectors were living in tents in Nome and twice that many participated in the Alaska gold rush. Many Inuit came to the area in the summer seeking employment. Miners were paying up to $100 a day for people to help them carry their mining equipment to the gold fields.

Many of the Inuit who came to Nome ended up staying. It became the largest town in that part of Alaska. The prospectors eventually covered every inch of Alaska and found gold in other places as well in the early years of the 20th century. As it turned out, the land that had been called Seward's Folly by some is rich in natural resources. The exploitation of those resources starting with fur traders, followed by whalers and gold miners continues today with increasing demands for the oil that has been discovered in the Arctic regions of both Alaska and Canada. The removal of resources from the Arctic has often had a negative affect on the Inuit and other Native people of the north. Meeting the challenges of the 20th century caused suffering for many people in the Arctic.

7

The Twentieth Century in the Arctic

The 20th century was a time of great change throughout the world. Changes in technology have affected the lives of most people on Earth. Radios, movies, television, telephones, and now the Internet have dramatically changed how people communicate and exchange ideas. Cars, trains, modern ships, and airplanes have made even the remotest regions of the world familiar to many. At the beginning of the 20th century, there were Inuit groups that had still not had extensive contact with the outside world. By the end of the century, Inuit villages that were extremely isolated had satellite communication links that brought education and other information directly to them.

Many Arctic people struggled to survive during this century of immense change in their world. Fortunately, many have struck a balance that has allowed them to maintain their unique identities while incorporating aspects of the white world into their lives. At

In the 20th century, remote locations such as Baker Lake were able to import technology such as modern stoves. A man watches as Sandy Lunan kneels by an oven while baking bread in Baker Lake, Northwest Territories, Canada, in 1946. *(National Archives of Canada)*

77

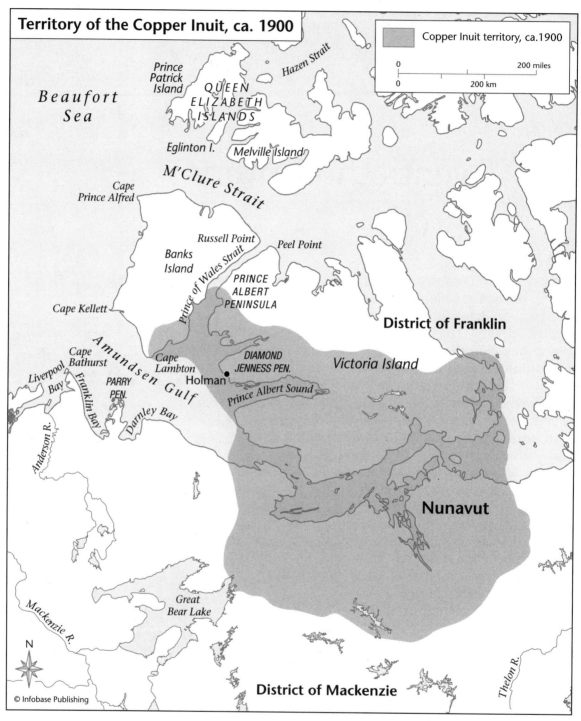

Territory of the Copper Inuit, ca. 1900

Copper Inuit territory, ca.1900

0   200 miles
0   200 km

Beaufort Sea

Prince Patrick Island

QUEEN ELIZABETH ISLANDS

Hazen Strait

Eglinton I.

Melville Island

M'Clure Strait

Cape Prince Alfred

Russell Point

Peel Point

Banks Island

Prince of Wales Strait

PRINCE ALBERT PENINSULA

Cape Kellett

District of Franklin

Amundsen Gulf

Cape Bathurst

Cape Lambton

DIAMOND JENNESS PEN.

Victoria Island

Liverpool Bay

Franklin Bay

PARRY PEN.

Holman

Prince Albert Sound

Darnley Bay

Anderson R.

Great Bear Lake

Nunavut

Mackenzie R.

N

District of Mackenzie

Thelon R.

© Infobase Publishing

It was not until the 20th century that the Copper Inuit of Canada had contact with whites. The impact of white culture on the Copper Inuit is well documented, as anthropologists recorded the changes to their traditional culture in the first half of the 20th century.

times, the governments of Canada and the United States seemed to be bent on the destruction of the Arctic people within their borders. This too has changed as governments have come to recognize and accept the idea of Native peoples living as equal citizens with different lifestyles and beliefs than the mainstream of modern society in North America. As the 20th century ended, there were many positive steps being made by the Aleut and Inuit of the Arctic.

THE LAST TO BE CONTACTED

Although most of the Arctic had been explored by whites in the 19th century, there was a group of Inuit in the central Arctic region of Canada who still lived a traditional lifestyle without the use of non-Native items. Anthropologists refer to these people as the Copper Inuit because of the use of copper in their tools. They live in the Arctic in an area from the point where the Perry River enters Queen Maud Sound west to the Dolphin and Union Strait. Prior to contact with whites in the early 1900s, they lived on both the mainland and the islands to the north, including Victoria Island and Banks Island.

Much of what we know of the Copper Inuit was recorded by Vilhjálmur Stefánsson and R. M. Anderson between 1908 and 1918. Prior to their exploration of the range of the Copper Inuit, much of the area and the people had been unknown to the outside world. By the 1920s, trading ships began visiting the Copper Inuit at Coronation Gulf and the lives of the Copper Inuit changed quickly. Nets, rifles, and traps quickly changed their hunting techniques and patterns. Canvas tents and cloth clothing for summer wear were also adopted.

The Copper Inuit had lived the traditional life of moving out on the ice in the winter and hunting seals at breathing holes. With the use of rifles, they began staying inland, hunting caribou and trapping. The story of the Copper Inuit mirrors that of most Arctic people but is better documented as it happened in a very brief period of time when scientists were frequently coming to the Arctic to record the story of the Inuit. Missionaries, fur traders, and the Canadian government through the Royal Canadian Mounted Police all contributed to the end of the traditional lifestyle of the Copper Inuit. The Copper Inuit also experienced an influx of Inuit from the west. It is assumed that these hunters had depleted the animal resources in their traditional territories and wanted to take advantage of the underutilized resources of the Copper region.

The 20th century brought new resources and technological methods to the Inuit and Aleut. A resident of Yukon Territory mends a dog harness in this 1981 photograph. *(U.S. Fish and Wildlife Service)*

These western Inuit had already adapted to nontraditional goods and hunting techniques and contributed to the "modernization" of the Copper Inuit. The Copper Inuit were soon living in fewer and larger communities. They gave up the kayak for imported wooden canoes and boats. By the 1950s, the number of caribou in the area had been greatly reduced, forcing people back to the ocean to hunt seals. Many Inuit, including some in the Copper region, became construction workers for a brief period of time. In the 1950s, the governments of Canada and the United States cooperated on the building of the Distant Early Warning (DEW) Line—a series of radar stations that were intended to protect North America from attack by planes flying in from the Soviet Union.

THE REINDEER EXPERIMENT

For many years, the U.S. government tried to impose its will on Native people throughout its territory. Education was made mandatory and children were forced to speak only English at school. In addition, many groups were forced to change their lifestyles in hopes that they would become part of the mainstream culture of the United States. Many Indians in the Lower 48, as the contiguous 48 states are called by Alaskans, had been forced onto reservations that were sometimes far from their original homes. The government introduced many programs that were designed to end traditional ways of living. Plains Indians who had followed the buffalo herds and lived as hunters were forced

THE DEW LINE

After World War II, the countries of North America and western Europe entered into what was called the cold war with the Union of Soviet Socialist Republics (USSR or Soviet Union), which was Russia and all the countries it controlled. The greatest fear of the cold war was that the two most powerful countries militarily of the time—the United States and the Soviet Union—would end up in a war against each other during which nuclear weapons would be used. Military experts in the United States were concerned that the Soviet Union's bombers could fly over the Arctic and attack the United States. Radar stations that had been built along the Canadian/U.S. border would not provide enough warning to stop an attack.

In the early 1950s, the idea of building a series of radar stations across the Arctic was devised. Between 1953 and 1957, 60 radar stations were built across the Arctic from Alaska to Baffin Island. Many Inuit worked as laborers on these sites. Each site required an airport, power plant, housing for staff, as well as the radar station. The effectiveness of the DEW Line ended with the introduction of intercontinental ballistic missiles in 1962. However, the money earned by the Inuit helped many purchase more modern equipment.

to be farmers. In the Northwest, Indians who had survived for thousands of years as fishermen, lost the lands along the rivers they had fished.

In Alaska, the government wanted to change the lifestyle of the Inuit. The climate of the Arctic made it impossible for them to become farmers. So, the government decided to try to make the Inuit ranchers. Cattle and other traditional farm animals would never be able to survive in the Arctic. However, in the Arctic regions of Scandinavia, the people who lived there known as Lapps had become very successful at keeping herds of reindeer. In the early years of the 20th century, large numbers of reindeer were imported into Alaska.

The government believed that reindeer would make up for the

Religious education attempted to assimilate people of the Arctic into mainstream North American culture. Father Trinell, surrounded by Inuit children, stands in the doorway of a Roman Catholic mission in Cape Dorset, Northwest Territories (now Nunavut), in 1951. *(National Archives of Canada)*

Reindeer graze within the confines of a corral on Nunivak Island, Alaska. In the early 20th century, the U.S. government planned to force the Inuit to become ranchers of reindeer imported from Norway. *(U.S. Fish and Wildlife Service)*

loss of caribou and sea mammals that had been depleted by overhunting. Many Inuit did not take to the job of tending herds of reindeer. For the most part, the introduction of reindeer did not accomplish the goal of creating an agriculture-based economy for the Inuit. By the 1970s, there were still almost 20,000 reindeer in 12 Inuit-owned herds on Seward Peninsula.

ALASKA NATIVE CLAIMS SETTLEMENT ACT (ANCSA)

When the United States bought Alaska from Russia in 1867, the treaty called for the protection of the Aleut, Inuit, and other Native people who lived there. The treaty also called for the recognition of Alaska Natives' land rights, but the United States did little to live up to that promise. It allowed whalers, fur traders, miners, and later homesteaders open access to Alaska. When Alaska became a state in 1959, the Native people of the state received somewhat better treatment than they had under the federal government. The state integrated schools that had been segregated since 1911. However, the state was allowed to select 104 million acres from the lands claimed by the federal government to become state land.

The state share of the open land in Alaska amounted to one-third of the state. The land selected was the best available and the state did not compensate any Alaska Natives for the land they took. A large number of land claims resulted because both the state and federal governments ignored the prior claims that

Richfield Oil rig stands, covered in snow, on the Kenai Peninsula of Alaska in 1958. The discovery of oil in Alaska in 1957 led that territory to become a state in 1959—changing the government of the Inuit once again. *(Anchorage Museum)*

TUNDRA TIMES

In 1958, the U.S. Atomic Energy Commission (AEC) planned to deepen a harbor on Cape Thompson in northwest Alaska using an atomic explosion. They felt this would be a good test of using nuclear power for peaceful means. They assured the local people that it would cause no harm. Many Inuit in the area were opposed to the idea of an atomic bomb being exploded in their backyard. In fall 1961, leaders from 20 Inuit communities came together to see what could be done to stop the plans of the AEC. One of the problems that faced the people who attended that conference was the difficulty of getting word out on Alaska Native issues. It was suggested at that time that the Alaska Natives needed their own newspaper. The AEC gave up their plan to explode a bomb in Alaska, but the idea of an Alaska Native newspaper stuck.

Howard Rock, an Inuit artist from Point Hope who was home from Seattle, where he had a studio, was convinced to edit the paper and Tom Snapp, a white journalist who had been sensitive to Native issues was recruited as the only reporter. The first issue of the paper went out on October 1, 1962. The *Tundra Times* became the voice of the Alaska Natives when they were

Howard Rock, Theodore Hetzel, and Tom Snapp (from left to right) stand by a table that holds printer's type blocks in 1959. Howard Rock and Tom Snapp collaborated to produce the *Tundra Times,* a newspaper that focuses on Alaska Native issues. *(University of Alaska, Fairbanks)*

being ignored by the mainstream press. During the arguments between Alaska Native groups prior to the ANCSA, the *Tundra Times* is credited with helping to unify the issues that confronted Alaskan Natives. Although the circulation of the paper has never been very large, its influence has been felt throughout Alaska and all the way to Washington, D.C.

Alaska Natives had to the land. Those claims might have gone unanswered if oil had not been discovered on the North Slope of Alaska.

In 1966, a number of Native groups formed the Alaska Federation of Natives (AFN) to pursue their land claims against the state and federal governments. The discovery of oil in the Alaska Arctic and the desire to build a pipeline to bring the oil from Prudhoe Bay on the Arctic Ocean to Valdez (a port in southwest Alaska that remains ice free much of the year) gave the AFN the leverage they needed to push for

In fall 1970, Secretary of the Interior Walter Hickel (seated at desk) met with individuals involved in the Alaska land claims dispute. Later the same year, Congress passed the Alaska Native Claims Settlement Act (ANCSA), which was designed to distribute land and money to Alaska Natives. *(Alaska State Library)*

a settlement of their land claims. Both the oil fields in the Arctic and the route of the proposed pipeline crossed through land claimed by Alaska Natives. As the AFN prepared to fight for a settlement, they were confronted by numerous differing opinions among the people they represented. One of the unifying voices during this time was the *Tundra Times,* a Native Alaskan newspaper.

With the increased demand for oil in the United States the U.S. Congress stepped in to try and clear the way for the development of the oil fields and pipeline. In 1971, the U.S. Congress passed the Alaska Natives Claim Settlement Act (ANCSA). The ANCSA designated 44 million acres of Alaska for Native Alaskans. It also agreed to pay $962.5 million to settle all claims.

The money was to be paid over 11 years and would go to 200 village and 13 regional corporations. The corporations were given numerous instructions as to what could be done with the money. Some had to be invested in profitable businesses that would benefit the Alaska Natives who were made shareholders. Some of the money could be invested in nonprofit businesses that would benefit the shareholders. The corporations were also allowed to distribute part of the money directly to their shareholders.

Although there has been some controversy among shareholders about the operation of the corporations, numerous economic opportunities have come about for Alaska Natives because of ANCSA. This, too, has caused controversy as some have claimed that the corporations have forced more people away from their traditional life.

HYDRO-QUÉBEC

Alaska was not the only place where governments had to interact with Native people so they could develop sources of energy. In 1971, the province of Québec came up with a plan to build a huge power project in James Bay (a part of Hudson Bay). When built, the project would provide power to much of the province as well as enabling them to sell power to the United States. The project called for numerous dams and drastic changes to the landscape of the area. The area that would be included in the project was part of the traditional hunting grounds of both Inuit and Cree groups.

The Cree took the project to court and won a temporary halt to the plan. As a result, in 1975 a land claim settlement was negotiated with the Inuit and Cree of James Bay. In exchange for the Inuit and Cree giving up their claims to the 140,000 square miles that would be affected, they received claim to the lands around their communities, hunting rights over an extensive area, and $225 million. It was the first settlement of a land claim in Canada after the creation of an Office of Native Claims. Although the settlement seemed like a lot of money to many, some Inuit and Cree were not pleased. They felt that there was no amount of money that could compensate for the loss of this huge area forever.

INUIT CIRCUMPOLAR CONFERENCE

The 1970s saw a growing awareness of Inuit activism across the Arctic. The Inuit of Alaska had been involved in the Alaska Native

Claims Settlement Act. The Inuit of Québec were involved in the fight with Hydro-Québec. The Inuit of Canada formed the Inuit Tapirisat of Canada to further Inuit issues. In 1971, a group of Inuit in Greenland organized Siumut (Forward) to fight for home rule and other Inuit issues with Denmark. Other groups also sprang up at this time. In 1973, Greenland Inuit based in Copenhagen called for an Arctic Peoples Conference.

Canadian and Greenland Inuit met at the Copenhagen conference but no one from Alaska or Russia attended. However, many across the Arctic felt the idea of a united Inuit voice was a good one. The Inuit, Eben Hopson, who was the mayor of Barrow, Alaska, took on the task of laying the groundwork for a pan-Inuit council. Due to the distances involved and the lack of regular transportation across the Arctic at the time, the only way to fly from Greenland to Alaska was via Denmark. It took more than two years for the first meetings to be held.

Eben Hopson, pictured here in a 1959 portrait, was instrumental in organizing the first Inuit Circumpolar Conference (ICC). The ICC brings Inuit from Alaska, Canada, Greenland, and Russia together in meetings to develop policies for the Arctic region. *(Alaska State Library)*

In March 1976, the first meetings were held in Alaska with representatives from Greenland, Canada, and Alaska in attendance. During the 1976 meeting, plans were finalized for the first Inuit Circumpolar assembly. From June 13 to 16, 1977, 18 Inuit delegates from each of the three countries met in Barrow. In addition, the meeting attracted 300 observers from the press and other organizations. The major accomplishment of the meeting was the creation of the Inuit Circumpolar Conference (ICC). Plans were made to create a charter and to hold further meetings.

It was almost four years before a charter could be agreed upon by all the different groups involved. One obstacle was

GREENLAND HOME RULE

Since the first Norse colonists arrived in Greenland more than 1,000 years ago, Denmark has considered Greenland part of its territory. In some ways, the Inuit of Greenland fared better than the Inuit in other parts of the Arctic. However, in the 1970s, they were still ruled from Copenhagen and the Greenland Provincial Assembly had little authority. The Siumut and other Inuit political parties in Greenland began to petition the government for more local control.

In 1972, the Provincial Assembly formally came out in support of home rule. A commission was created in 1975 and negotiations began with the government in Denmark. On November 29, 1978, the Greenland Home Rule Act was passed in Denmark. It called for a transfer of control of Greenland over a period of five years. At the end of that time, Greenlanders would control their own political fate while still being a part of the Danish commonwealth. Greenlanders still depend on financial support from Denmark and a complete break was not really practical.

the fight for home rule in Greenland. The final charter was presented to the Second Inuit Circumpolar Conference held in Gothåb, Greenland, in 1980. It passed unanimously. Since that time, the ICC has been at the forefront of issues that affect the Inuit and the Arctic.

Throughout the remainder of the 20th century, the ICC grew as a voice for the people of the Arctic. During that time, the Inuit of Russia joined the ICC. Some members of the organization hoped for a separate Inuit country that spanned the Arctic. Although an Inuit country is unlikely, the idea of more local control has spread across the region. Inuit self-determination has been most successful in Canada with the creation of Nunavut.

NUNAVUT

As early as 1977, members of the Inuit Tapirisat of Canada called for the division of the Canadian Northwest Territories into two separate provinces so that the mainly Inuit population in the eastern half of the area would gain more local control of the political and social systems that affected their lives. They suggested that this new province be called Nunavut (Our Land).

Nunavut Territory, Canada, April 1, 1999

Greenland
(DENMARK)

Beaufort Sea

Baffin
Bay

Taloyoak
(Spence Bay)

Nunavut

Northwest
Territories

Iqaluit

Baker Lake

Rankin
Inlet

Arviat

Hudson
Bay

Alberta

C A N A D A

N

Saskatchewan

Manitoba

Québec

James
Bay

Ontario

0   500 miles

0   500 km

© Infobase Publishing

On April 1, 1999, the Nunavut territory was created as a separate province of Canada, including a large territory of Hudson Bay and all the islands to the north and in Hudson Bay. Nunavut's population is mostly Inuit.

In a ceremony to commemorate the creation of the territory of Nunavut in April 1999, performers and Inuit Junior Rangers assemble around flags representing the ten provinces and three territories of Canada. The creation of Nunavut allowed for greater self-government and self-determination for the Inuit of northern Canada. *(AP Images)*

Over the next 20 years, many Inuit came to support the idea. In 1982, the government of the Northwest Territories held a special vote to see how people felt about Nunavut. The Inuit voted overwhelmingly for the split. The white voters in the Territories voted against it. However, when the votes from both groups were tallied, 56 percent of the people voting favored the creation of Nunavut. From that point on, negotiations proceeded with the Canadian federal government.

The basis of the Nunavut movement was a land claim case brought by the group known as the Tungavik Federation of Nunavut. The ultimate creation of Nunavut was a part of the settlement of that land claim. The land claim settlement was signed by all parties involved on May 25, 1993. It called for the creation of the Nunavut territory of 136,000 square miles that includes the eastern part of what was the Northwest Territories, the Arctic islands to the north and east including Baffin Island and all the islands in Hudson Bay.

The agreement also created a political structure for Nunavut and provided a transfer of more than $1.148 billion (Canadian) over 14 years. On April 1, 1999, political control of Nunavut was passed to the elected officials of the territory that include a premier and a 19-member legislature. The population of Nunavut is spread across this vast territory and lives primarily in 28 small communities. As of July 2000, there were 27,692 people in Nunavut and close to 60 percent of them consider themselves Inuit. Nunavut stands as an example of self-determination to Inuit and other Native Americans and has already become a center for the preservation of Inuit culture.

8

The Arctic Peoples Today

As the 21st century begins, the Inuit and Aleut people of the Arctic have made great strides in standing up for their rights and taking control of their futures. However, they still face many challenges in the years ahead. According to recent census figures in Canada, the United States, and Greenland, there are more than 138,000 Inuit still living in the Arctic. In addition, there are more than 10,000 Aleut living in Alaska. Some of the greatest challenges many of these people face are caused by the encroachment of modern society in the north. Oil and other natural resource development have brought many non-Natives to the Arctic while many Inuit have ended up as laborers in mines and oil fields.

In addition, technology has come to the north in the form of satellite communications, bringing white education into even the most remote corners of the Arctic. Education is a double-edged sword for many people in the Arctic. Many believe people need to be educated to deal with the outside world and to bring opportunities to their own communities. However, learning English is often done at the cost of losing much or all of the local Inuit and Aleut dialects. For the people of the Arctic, their culture exists within the ability of their languages to express it. Realizing this, many groups have undertaken projects to preserve their languages and to insure that young people have the opportunity to learn their language. Technology may be the key to saving the languages of the Arctic. Textbooks in Inupiaq and Aleut do not exist. However, many young students in the Arctic have computers and know how to use them. Computer-based language programs help students learn their traditional

Houses and satellite dishes mark the landscape of Arctic Village, Alaska, about 200 miles north of the Arctic Circle. Technological inventions such as satellite dishes and the Internet have drastically altered the traditional lifestyle of Arctic people while improving their communication with the rest of the world. *(AP Images)*

languages along with the regular curriculum that is beamed into their remote communities via satellite. The fact that the people of the Arctic are taking responsibility for education in their communities rather than being dictated to by some distant government agency is allowing for increased learning of traditional language and culture.

GLOBAL WARMING

For the people of the Arctic who are trying to maintain a modified form of their traditional lifestyles, the affects of global warming may cause more trouble than all the fur traders, missionaries, and whalers combined. Throughout the history of the world, there have been periods of time when the Earth was both colder and warmer than it is now. The most recent example of this is the ice age that existed at the time the first American

Indians crossed Beringia from Asia to North America. Since that time, the Earth has been slowly getting warmer.

Many scientists believe that the emissions from modern industry and vehicles have accelerated the process of the Earth's warming. They state that the gases in these emissions are polluting the atmosphere and turning the Earth into a large greenhouse that does not release as much heat into space as it once did. The people of the Arctic are noticing the change in their environment whether greenhouse gases are contributing or not.

According to the Inuit Circumpolar Conference (ICC) website (http://www.inuitcircumpolar.com), people living in the Arctic and Subarctic regions have noticed numerous changes to their environment due to global warming. One complaint common to people across the Canadian Arctic is that the sky has changed color and is hazy much of the time. They have also noticed a reduction in the permafrost that has caused landslides as well as damage to houses, roads, pipelines, and other natural and human-made structures. There has also been a substantial loss of land along the coast. In Shishmaref, Alaska, on the Chukchi Sea, rising sea levels have caused three houses to fall into the sea and seven others have been relocated. Engineers have predicted that within 20 years the entire community of 600 houses will be inundated by sea water.

Already people have discovered that the elusive Northwest Passage, which remained a frozen secret for hundreds of years is now easily passable in the summers. In summer 2000, Canadian Mountie Ken Burton cautiously headed north to explore the Northwest Passage in a 65-foot aluminum patrol boat. Much to his surprise, the passage was ice-free and he was able to travel through over a three-week period. Some have predicted that within 50 years, the Northwest Passage could become a northern version of the Panama Canal with ships using it as it was originally imagined—a summer short cut for ships carrying goods from Europe to Asia and back. The potential for oil spills and other contamination of the Arctic Ocean has many people worried.

In addition, scientists have observed a reduction in the extent and thickness of sea ice. These changes are affecting the quantity and location of animals that many Arctic people still depend on to survive. Whales are traveling farther offshore, making it much harder to hunt them. The bowhead whale is

Seals cover the rocks of Zapadni Rookery on St. George Island in the Pribilof Islands in the Bering Sea in this 2002 photograph. The introduction of commercial hunting in the Arctic and worsening environmental conditions are responsible for a dramatic decline in the population of seals and other animals that used to populate the Arctic region. *(U.S. Fish and Wildlife Service)*

the most important for the subsistence hunting of many Arctic people. In the 21st century, whale hunting has become even more controversial as it has become an international political issue for conservationists and the International Whaling Commission (IWC), which in 2002 banned further whaling by the Inuit. Some Inuit who depended on whales for as much as 60 percent of their annual food have continued to whale in spite of the ban. In 2005, Canada moved to create the first marine sanctuary for whales. When negotiations with the province of Nunavut are concluded, the waters of Isabella Bay will be a sanctuary for approximately 300 bowheads whales that summer there. It is believed that the once threatened population now stands at over 8,000 bowheads worldwide. In the Pribilof Islands, the fur seal population has dramatically dropped from more than 2.5 million 50 years ago to approximately 800,000 seals today. Large-scale commercial hunting of these seals was stopped in 1911 and Aleut hunters are restricted to harvesting fewer than 1,000 seals a year. Although no one is willing to say for sure, many suspect changes in the environment for the continued decline of the fur seals in the Pribilof Islands and other sea mammals like the Steller sea lions, which are now an endangered species.

SHEILA WATT-CLOUTIER
(1953–   )

Sheila Watt-Cloutier was born in Kuujjuaq, Nunavik (northern Quebec), on December 2, 1953. Watt-Cloutier spent her early childhood living the traditional Inuit life. As with many Inuit children at the time, she was sent away from her family to go to school. She attended schools in Nova Scotia and Churchill, Manitoba, before enrolling at McGill University in Montreal. At McGill, she studied education and counseling. When she left college, she worked at Ungava Hospital located in her hometown—the largest community in northern Quebec although it has fewer than 2,000 people.

In the early 1990s, she worked in the education department and was one of the people responsible for an influential report on the education system of Northern Quebec. She also took a significant part in the creation of a video intended to create cultural awareness for young people. The video is entitled *Capturing Spirit: The Inuit Journey*. In 1995, Watt-Cloutier was elected president of the Canadian branch of the ICC. In 2002, she became the chair of the executive board of the ICC, and she has been a tireless crusader for all issues that impact the Inuit people across the Arctic. In 2005, she was awarded the Sophie Prize, which yearly recognizes people making a significant contribution to international environmental and development issues. In February 2007, Watt-Cloutier was nominated for a Nobel Peace Prize.

Sheila Watt-Cloutier holds the 2005 Sophie Prize and poses for a photograph with Norwegian Minister of Environment Knut Arild Hareide in Oslo, Norway, on June 15, 2005. Watt-Cloutier has been an advocate for the Inuit and chairwoman of the Inuit Circumpolar Conference. *(AP Images)*

A woman travels on a dogsled in Togiak National Wildlife Refuge in Alaska in 2004. The traditional way of life of the Inuit is threatened by climate change, which is responsible for melting ice in the Arctic. *(U.S. Fish and Wildlife Service)*

Groups like the ICC and their dynamic chair, Sheila Watt-Cloutier, have been in the forefront of trying to make the world aware of the environmental crisis in the Arctic. Watt-Cloutier has traveled to conferences around the world presenting the case that changes in the Arctic environment are real and a threat to the people who live there.

For the Inuit, global warming means much more than warmer summers and shorter winters. The ability of people to continue to subsist in the Arctic is still based on the availability of traditional animals and fish for food. Without the traditional aspects of Inuit life, Inuit culture will be in jeopardy. Some have argued that changes in the Arctic environment are a warning of what the rest of the world can expect if steps are not taken to reduce or even reverse global human contributions to global warming.

OIL IN THE ARCTIC

The discovery of oil on the North Slope of Alaska was the event that forced the U.S. government to negotiate the Alaska Native Claims Settlement Act. Ongoing revenues from the wells at Prudhoe Bay and elsewhere have helped lift many Alaska

ARCTIC NATIONAL WILDLIFE REFUGE (ANWR)

The Arctic National Wildlife Refuge was created in the 1950s by President Dwight Eisenhower. It consists of 19.5 million acres and is the largest wilderness remaining in North America. When the refuge was created, 1.5 million acres were set aside for future oil and gas exploration. This area is along the coast of the Arctic Ocean.

The Arctic National Wildlife Refuge includes the calving grounds of the Porcupine caribou herd. In addition to the caribou, the refuge is home to a number of unique Arctic

The threat of irreparable environmental destruction has caused environmentalists and many others to rally against oil exploration in the Arctic National Wildlife Refuge. An aerial photograph from 2001 depicts destruction of the Earth from oil exploration. *(U.S. Fish and Wildlife Service)*

Natives out of poverty. The existing oil fields are reaching the point where oil production is beginning to fall off. There are currently three major areas in Alaska where scientists believe there are large reserves of oil.

The fight over opening new oil fields has created an ongoing dilemma for many in Alaska and beyond. The best known of the

Many Inuit depend on the caribou for meat and thus oppose the destruction of land by oil exploration in the Arctic National Wildlife Refuge. Here a woman cuts up caribou meat in the refuge. *(U.S. Fish and Wildlife Service)*

plants and animals. Many environmentalists fear that oil drilling will adversely affect the caribou and other sensitive segments of the Arctic ecology. The environmentalists have found allies among the Gwich'in Indians who live south of the refuge and are very dependent on the Porcupine caribou for their subsistence. Many representatives from the Gwich'in, an Athapascan group who did not benefit from the Alaska Native Claims Settlement Act, have made their way to Washington, D.C., on many occasions to speak out against the development of oil and gas reserves in the Arctic National Wildlife Refuge.

areas is a part of the Arctic National Wildlife Refuge (ANWR). The other two areas are the National Petroleum Reserve at Teshekpuk Lake and the Yukon Flats National Wildlife Refuge. All three areas are sensitive and unique habitats for a variety of Arctic species. Whether to drill in any or all of these areas has forced many to choose sides.

The modern snowmobile and the traditional dogsled pictured here in Huslia Village, Alaska, point to the Inuit's conflict between traditional and modern lifestyles. *(U.S. Fish and Wildlife Service)*

President George W. Bush and many Republicans have fought to open oil drilling in ANWR. Allied with them have been a number of groups representing Inuit who would benefit from the development of additional oil fields. One of the regional corporations set up under the Alaska Native Claims Settlement Act, Arctic Slope Regional Corp., actually owns the mineral rights to almost 100,000 acres within the refuge. The leaders of Arctic Slope have been lobbying hard for the opening of ANWR. They say that environmentalists who have never been to the Arctic should not have the right to prevent the people who have lived there for thousands of years from benefiting from the increased demand for oil.

The money Arctic Slope and its Inuit shareholders would receive would insure their ability to continue to live in the Arctic without getting welfare from the state and federal government. Similar arguments have been put forth by other Inuit groups over drilling in the other areas. When the U.S. Congress passed the Energy Bill in summer 2005, the House of Representatives had included drilling in ANWR, however it was taken out by the Senate and was not in the final bill.

By 2007, gas and oil prices reached record highs. This puts more pressure on developing known oil reserves in the United States and Canada. In Nunavut, there are also known reserves of gas and oil. However, the cost of getting that oil out of the ground was not economically feasible when oil was selling at less than $40 a barrel. Now that crude oil is selling at more than $90 a barrel, the Inuit of Nunavut may also face the dilemma presented by oil development. They will have to balance the economic benefits against the environmental damage.

ART AND CULTURAL RENAISSANCE

Since the first Europeans came in contact with the people of the Arctic, the carving and other artistic expressions of the Inuit and Aleut have been in demand by the outside world. During the later years of the 20th century, many Native artists formed cooperatives that were involved in marketing Inuit and Aleut art. Carvings in bone, stone, and ivory as well as a number of other craft items became highly sought after. Numerous carvers have become well known as their work has been sold throughout North America and beyond.

With the support of the Nunavut government and many of the Alaska Native corporations, the arts have flourished in the north. Along with traditional arts, there has been an increase in written and film expressions of Arctic culture. One of the most celebrated of these is the first feature length movie filmed in Inuit. *Atanarjuat (The Fast Runner)* is a 2001 film about a group of Inuit living a traditional lifestyle at some point in the past. The movie chronicles the conflicts that arise between members of the group who want to control the group. The movie gives the viewer

Repulse Bay co-op worker Teresa Kingurk displays carved antlers in this 1971 photograph. Artists' cooperatives have been a way for people of the Arctic to sell and publicize their work—raising awareness of Inuit and Aleut culture in the process. *(Northwest Territories)*

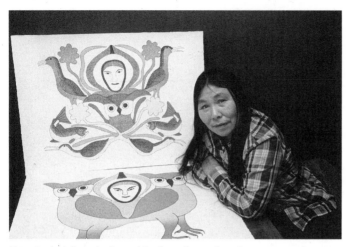

Kenojuak Ashevak, famed Inuit artist and sculptor, poses by two of her artworks in this 1980 photograph. Ashevak has received numerous awards and honors for her work, including becoming a Companion of the Order of Canada in 1982. *(National Archives of Canada)*

an interesting look into the traditional lives of the Inuit of Igloolik.

The movie is based on an ancient Inuit legend that reaches back 4,000 years. It involves many aspects of traditional Inuit life. All of the actors and 80 percent of the film crew were Inuit. To try and place the film in the precontact period, the film crew used the journals and drawings from Admiral William Perry's expedition to Igloolik in the 1820s. The film is not only an artistic success in its portrayal of traditional Inuit culture; it has been a financial success in both North America and Europe.

ZACHARIAS KUNUK
(1958–)

Zacharias Kunuk, the director of *Atanarjuat*, was born in 1958 in Igloolik, Nunavut, Canada. Until he reached the age of nine, Kunuk lived the traditional life of the Inuit. At that time, his family was forced by the Canadian government to move into Igloolik, an Inuit community of 1,200 people, where the young Kunuk was required to attend school and learn English. Igloolik had a movie theater and Kunuk would carve wooden sculptures to earn the 25 cents needed to get into the movies. He has said that most of the movies played at that theater were westerns with actors like John Wayne killing Indians.

Taken by the movies, Kunuk sold a number of sculptures in Montreal in 1980 and used the money to buy a video camera. It was the first one in the town of Igloolik, and he began

shooting a video of his home and the people who lived there. His first attempt at a dramatic film was called *Qaggiq / Gathering Place* and was shot in 1989. During the 1990s, he made three other short dramatic pieces and two documentaries on the Inuit that were well received in Nunavut and beyond. At the end of the 1990s, he received a grant of $2 million from the Aboriginal Film-making Program of the National Film Board of Canada and began work on the full-length movie *Atanarjuat (The Fast Runner)*. When the film was presented in 2001 at the Cannes (France) Film Festival, it won the Golden Camera Award for first-time film directors. Kunuk's next movie will show the events of the first European missionaries and traders coming among the Inuit.

THE FUTURE

The concerns over natural resource development and global warming trouble many in the Arctic. However, the creation of Nunavut, the impending settlement of land claims for the Inuit of Quebec, the progress made by many of the Alaska Native corporations, and home rule in Greenland are all positive steps for the Aleut and Inuit. The growing voices of organizations like the Inuit Circumpolar Conference continue to be heard by government officials in the halls of capitals around the world. The people of the Arctic do not yet have the same standard of living as most people in North America but they are making gains.

A major accomplishment of many Arctic people is their growing ability to strike a balance between their culture and traditions and what is called the modern world. The Aleut and Inuit have survived for thousands of years in one of the harshest environments on the planet. This ability to survive will see them into the future.

Quebec premier Bernard Landry walks between two Inuit children after visiting a school in Tasiujaq, Quebec, on April 9, 2002. The province of Quebec continues to negotiate with Inuit regarding land claims and other issues important to the population. *(AP Images)*

≇ Time Line ≸

≈ 25,000 B.C.
Evidence found along the Old Crow River in Canada dated earliest-known humans in North America to this time.

≈ 25,000 B.C. to 5,000 B.C.
Archaeologists call this period Paleo Archaic or Stage 1.

≈ 5,000 B.C. to 2,200 B.C.
Two separate areas of culture, Ocean Bay I and the Northern Archaic culture, develop during what is called Stage 2 in the Arctic.

≈ 2,200 B.C. to 1,200 B.C.
During what is called Stage 3 in the Arctic, the two groups who became the Inuit and Aleut develop.

≈ 1,200 B.C. to A.D. 600
During Stage 4, the people of the Arctic settle in larger and more permanent villages.

≈ A.D. 600 to 1800
The Thule tradition develops in Stage 5.

≈ 985
It is believed that Eric the Red from Norway arrives in Greenland.

≈ 1300s
It is believed that all traces of the Scandinavians disappear.

≈ 1576
British captain Martin Frobisher sails into the Canadian Arctic, capturing three Inuit.

1585 and 1586

Englishman John Davis leads expeditions to the Arctic.

1648

Russian traders cross the Bering Sea and arrive in North America.

1670

The Hudson's Bay Company, a trading organization devoted to Far North goods and resources, is founded.

1721

Scandinavians led by Hans Egede establish a mission to convert the Inuit of Greenland.

1728

Russian Vitus Bering is first sent by Czar Peter the Great to explore the Arctic region.

1762

The Russians reach Kodiak Island.

1774–90

The Spanish send expeditions to Alaska in response to Russian settlements.

1778

British captain James Cook maps much of the coastline of Alaska and the Aleutian Islands.

1781

A smallpox epidemic wipes out 90 percent of the Natives in Churchill on the shores of Hudson Bay.

1782

The Instruction of 1782, regulations from Denmark to rule Greenland, are established.

1784

The Inuit fight a group of Russians on Kodiak Island.

1868

The United States buys Alaska from Russia.

1896

Gold is discovered in the Yukon Territory in Canada, setting off a major gold rush.

1898

Gold is discovered on Seward Peninsula in Alaska.

1903–06
Norwegian Roald Amundsen navigates the Northwest Passage.

1922
The film *Nanook of the North,* which documents life in the Arctic, is released.

1937
Reindeer Act of 1937 restricts ownership of domesticated reindeer to Native people.

1953–57
Canada and the United States cooperate on building the DEW Line, which consisted of 60 radar stations across the Arctic.

1959
Alaska becomes a state, which brings about better treatment of Alaskan Natives.

1961
Twenty Inuit communities came together to block an Atomic Energy Commission plan to use an atomic explosion to deepen the harbor at Cape Thompson, Alaska.

1962
The first issue of the *Tundra Times* is published.

1966
The Alaska Federation of Natives (AFN) is formed.

1969
The *Manhattan* becomes the first modern ship to travel from Alaska to the Atlantic.

1971
The U.S. Congress passes the Alaska Native Claims Settlement Act.
Inuit in Greenland form the organization Siumut (Forward) to help fight for home rule.

1975
A land claim settlement is reached between the Canadian government and the Inuit and the Cree.

1977
Inuit from the United States, Canada, and Greenland meet at the first Inuit Circumpolar assembly in Copenhagen, Denmark.

1978

The Greenland Home Rule Act is passed in Denmark.

1980

Members at the Second Inuit Circumpolar Conference agree on a charter.

1993

As part of a land claim settlement, Nunavut Territory is established.

1999

Control of Nunavut Territory is passed to newly elected officials.

2005

The U.S. Congress votes not to open up oil drilling in the Arctic National Wildlife Refuge.

2007

Canadian Inuit leader Sheila Watt-Cloutier is nominated for a Nobel Peace Prize.

Historical Sites and Museums

CANADA
Labrador

HOPEDALE

Hopedale National Historic Site of Canada Moravian missionaries arrived at the Inuit community of Arvertok in 1782. The daily life of the Inuit and the Moravians in the 19th century is displayed at the Hopedale Mission.

> **Address:** Agvituk Historical Society, P.O. Box 161, Hopedale, Labrador, Canada A0P 1G0
> **Web Site:** www.pc.gc.ca/voyage-travel/pv-vp/itm1-/page16_e.asp

Northwest Territorities

INUVIK

Ivvavik National Park of Canada The Ivvavik National Park has archaeological sites that document 8,000 years of human history.

> **Address:** P.O. Box 1840, Inuvik, NWT, Canada X0E 0T0
> **Phone:** 867-777-8800
> **Web Site:** www.pc.gc.ca/pn-np/yt/ivvavik/natcul/index_E.asp

PAULATUK

Tuktut Nogait National Park of Canada There are more than 360 archaeological sites in the park, some dating back to A.D. 1000.

> **Address:** Box 91, Paulatuk, NWT, Canada X0E 1N0
> **Phone:** 867-580-3233
> **Web Site:** www.pc.gc.ca/pn-np/nt/tuktutnogait/natcul/natcul2_
> e.asp

SACHS HARBOUR

Aulavik National Park of Canada There are numerous archaeological sites at Aulavik National Park, from pre-Dorset times back to 1500 B.C. through the Thule period in A.D. 1450.

> **Address:** Box 29, Sachs Harbour, NWT, Canada X0E 0Z0
> **Phone:** 867-690-3904
> **Web Site:** www.pc.gc.ca/pn-np/nt/aulavik/natcul/natcul2_e.asp

Nunavut

CAPE DORSET

Mallikjuaq Territorial Park There are a number of archaeological sites on Mallikjuaq Island.

> **Address:** Mallikjuaq Visitor Centre, Cape Dorset, Baffin Island
>   Nunavut, Canada XOA OCO
> **Phone:** 867-897-8996
> **Web Site:** www.nunavutparks.com

IQALUIT

Sylvia Grinnell Territorial Park The park, which is located one kilometer from Iqaluit, Nunavut's capital, has numerous archaeological sites within its borders.

> **Address:** Unikkaarvik Visitor Centre, Iqaluit, NT, Canada X0A 0H0
> **Phone:** 819-979-4636
> **Web Site:** www.nunavutparks.com/on_the_land/
>   sylvia_grinnell_park.cfm

Québec

GATINEAU

Canadian Museum of Civilization The museum has several permanent exhibits on the culture and history of Canada's Native people.

> **Address:** P.O. Box 3100, Station B, 100 Laurier Street, Gatineau,
>   Québec, Canada J8X 4H2
> **Phone:** 800-555-5621
> **Web Site:** www.civilization.ca/cmc/genereng.html

QUÉBEC

Museé National des Beaux-Arts du Québec The museum recently has acquired the Brousseau collection of Inuit art, which was one of the largest private collections in Canada.

> **Address:** Parc des Champs-de-Bataille, Québec, Canada G1R 5H3
> **Phone:** 418-643-2150
> **Web Site:** www.mnba.qc.ca

GREENLAND

NUUK

Greenland National Museum The museum has numerous displays on Inuit history and culture.

> **Address:** Hans Egedevej 8, Postboks 145, 3900 Nuuk, Greenland
> **Phone:** 299-32-26-11
> **Web Site:** www.natmus.gl

UNITED STATES
Alaska

ANAKTUVUK PASS

Simon Paneak Memorial Museum The Simon Paneak Memorial Museum has exhibits on Nunamiut Inuit history and culture.

> **Address:** POB 21085, 341 Mekiana Road, Anaktuvuk Pass, AK 99721
> **Phone:** 907-661-3413
> **Web Site:** www.north-slope.org/nsb/55.htm

ANCHORAGE

Alaska Native Heritage Center The Alaska Native Heritage Center has both indoor exhibits and outdoor sites that introduce local residents and visitors to Native culture.

> **Address:** 8800 Heritage Center Drive, Anchorage, AK 99506
> **Phone:** 907-330-8000
> **Web Site:** www.alaskanative.net

Anchorage Museum of History and Art The museum has exhibits of Alaska Natives' history and art.

> **Address:** P.O. 196650, 121 West 7th Avenue, Anchorage, AK 99519-6650
> **Phone:** 907-343-4326
> **Web Site:** www.anchoragemuseum.org

BARROW

Inupiat Heritage Center The Inupiat Heritage Center has exhibits on Native history and culture.

> **Address:** Ilisagvik College, Barrow, AK 99723
> **Phone:** 800-478-7337
> **Web Site:** www.nps.gov/inup

FAIRBANKS

University of Alaska Museum of the North The museum has programs and exhibits on Native history.

Address: P.O. Box 756960, 907 Yukon Drive, Fairbanks, AK
99775-6960
Phone: 907-474-7505
Web Site: www.uaf.edu/museum/index.html

JUNEAU

Alaska State Museum The Alaska State Museum displays the culture of
the Native people of Alaska.

Address: 395 Whittier Street, Juneau, AK 99801-1718
Phone: 907-465-2901
Web Site: www.museums.state.ak.us

KENAI

Kenai Visitors and Cultural Center The cultural center has an extensive
collection of materials and exhibits including Aleut materials.

Address: 11471 Kenai Spur Highway, Kenai, AK 99611
Phone: 907-283-1991
Web Site: www.visitkenai.com

KODIAK

Alutiiq Museum and Archaeological Repository The Alutiiq Museum
has a large collection of Inuit artifacts.

Address: 215 Mission Road, Suite 101, Kodiak, AK 99615
Phone: 907-486-7004
Web Site: www.alutiiqmuseum.com

KOTZEBUE

NANA Museum of the Arctic The NANA Museum of the Arctic
(one of 12 regional development corporations in Alaska) has sto-
rytelling, exhibits, as well as Inuit dancing and blanket toss in the
summer.

Mailing Address: c/o Tour Arctic, 1001 E. Benson Boulevard,
Anchorage, AK 99508
Physical Address: 100 Shore Avenue, Kotzebue, AK 99501
Phone: 907-265-4157

NOME

Carrie M. McLain Memorial Museum The museum has exhibits on
Inuit culture.

Address: Box 53, 200 E. Front Street, Nome, AK 99762
Phone: 907-443-6630
Web Site: www.nomealaska.org

UNALASKA

Museum of the Aleutians The museum has exhibits that display the
history and culture of the Aleut.

Address: P.O. Box 648, Unalaska, AK 99685-0648
Phone: 907-581-5150
Web Site: www.aleutians.org

VALDEZ

Maxine and Jesse Whitney Museum The Maxine and Jesse Whitney Museum has numerous exhibits, including an Inupiaq Inuit village scene.

Address: P.O. Box 97, 300 Airport Road, Valdez Airport Terminal, Valdez, AK 99686
Phone: 907-834-1690

▌Further Reading▐

BOOKS

Ansary, Mir Tamim. *Arctic Peoples*. Des Plaines, Ill.: Heinemann, 2000.

Burgan, Michael. *Inuit*. Milwaukee, Wis.: Gareth Stevens, 2005.

Corriveau, Danielle. *The Inuit of Canada*. Minneapolis, Minn.: Lerner, 2002.

Damas, David, ed. *Arctic*. Volume 5, *Handbook of the North American Indians*. Washington, D.C.: Smithsonian Institution, 1984.

George, Charles. *The Inuit*. San Diego, Calif.: KidHaven Press, 2005.

Koestler-Graek, Rachel A. *The Inuit: Ivory Carvers of the Far North*. Mankato, Minn.: Blue Earth Books, 2004.

Santella, Andrew. *The Inuit*. New York: Children's Press, 2001.

Thompson, Linda. *People of the Northwest and Subarctic*. Vero Beach, Fla.: Rourke, 2004.

Williams, Suzanne. *The Inuit*. New York: Franklin Watts, 2003.

Wolfson, Evelyn. *Inuit Mythology*. Berkeley Heights, N.J.: Enslow, 2001.

WEB SITES

Alaska Native Knowledge Network. "Welcome to Alaska Native Cultural Resources: Alaska Native Cultural Resources: Aleut-Alutiiq-Unangan/s-Sugpiaq. Available online. URL: www.ankn.uaf.edu/aleut.html. Downloaded on August 16, 2005.

"Arctic Circle." Available online. URL: arcticcircle.uconn.edu. Updated July 8, 2005.

Inuit Circumpolar Conference. "Welcome to the Inuit Circumpolar Conference." Available online. URL: www.inuitcircumpolar.com. Downloaded on August 27, 2005.

"Inuit Tapiriit Kanatami (ITK): Canada's National Inuit Organization." Available online. URL: www.itk.ca. Updated on August 11, 2005.

Morrison, David. "The Inuvialuit of the Western Arctic from Ancient Times to 1902." Available online. URL: www.civilization.ca/aborig/inuvial/indexe.html. Updated on April 28, 2004.

U.S. Fish & Wildlife Service. "Arctic National Wildlife Refuge." Available online. URL: arctic.fws.gov/index.htm. Downloaded on August 16, 2005.

"Welcome to Nunavut." Available online. URL: www.polarnet.ca/polarnet/nunavut.htm. Downloaded on August 16, 2005.

Index

Page numbers in *italic* indicate photographs/illustrations. Page numbers in **boldface** indicate box features. Page numbers followed by *m* indicate maps. Page numbers followed by *g* indicate tables. Page numbers followed by *t* indicate time line entries.